In Christ,

I Thrive

by

Rev. Dr. Caron Allen

In Christ, I Thrive

Trilogy Christian Publishers A Wholly Owned Subsidiary of Trinity Broadcasting Network

2442 Michelle Drive Tustin, CA 92780

Rights Department, 2442 Michelle Drive, Tustin, CA 92780.

Trilogy Christian Publishing/TBN and colophon are trademarks of Trinity Broadcasting Network.

Cover design by: Sierra Deyoe (Trilogy Christian Publishing)

For information about special discounts for bulk purchases, please contact Trilogy Christian Publishing.

Trilogy Disclaimer: The views and content expressed in this book are those of the author and may not necessarily reflect the views and doctrine of Trilogy Christian Publishing or the Trinity Broadcasting Network.

Manufactured in the United States of America

10 9 8 7 6 5 4 3 2 1

Library of Congress Cataloging-in-Publication Data is available.

ISBN: 979-8-88738-266-1

E-ISBN: 979-8-88738-267-8

DEDICATION

This work is dedicated to my grandchildren and great-grandchildren, who are my constant inspiration.

GMa/Duchess loves you!

ACKNOWLEDGMENTS

I am grateful for the opportunity to recognize some of the extraordinary Christian women in my life. They are my maternal great-grandmother, Elizabeth Burdette (deceased); my maternal grandmother, Leslie Cain (deceased); my paternal grandmother, Laura Bell Gibson (deceased); my mother, Marilyn Hyde (deceased); my daughters, Marcia Wilson, Anitra Pledger and Jeana Morris; my sisters, Rebekah Marshall, Renee Gibson Canady (deceased), and Leslie Shelton; my adopted daughters, Rev. Sandra Graham, Eydie Samuel, and Rev. Jamie Johnson; my mentor, Dr. Marjorie Miles; my friends, Pastor Gwendolyn Thomas, Laura Brooks, and Rev. Savannah Jackson; my spiritual mothers, First Lady Viola Moraigna (deceased), Bernice Harper (deceased), Ella Guillory (deceased), and Georgia Bivens.

I am a better woman because of what I have learned from each of you and because of the love you have given me. Each of you has impacted my life tremendously! My constant prayer for you all is that the Lord bless you and keep you; the Lord make His face shine upon you and be gracious to you; the Lord lift up His countenance upon you and give you peace (Numbers 6:24–26).

TABLE OF CONTENTS

In Christ, I Thrive

Rev. Dr. Caron Allen

PREFACE

In 2014, I was honored to be asked to be a participant in the nine-teenth annual St. Martin Art Festival and Bookfair. I traveled to the island, and with the help of my good friend, who is from St. Martin, I was able to gain a very in-depth look at the people and conditions.

One day, while driving through what many would call "a ghetto," I was struck speechless by the sight of the most beautiful tree I had ever seen. It stood grand, stately, benevolently overlooking a crime-ridden, drug-infested, poverty-stricken neighborhood filled with dilapidated buildings. Yet this giant defiantly arose through the concrete and fearlessly aimed for the sky, stretching its wide branches upward and outward. The flowers that bloomed from the tree were a brilliant, flaming red-and-orange mixture in color; one moment, more red than orange, and the next moment, the other way around, depending on how the sun's rays struck it.

I was dumbfounded by its beauty and its audacity to be so big and vibrant and gorgeous while surrounded by so much ugliness. How dare it thrive! How dare it be everything God intended it to be in these circumstances? How could it be? Wasn't it hindered, handi-capped, and stifled by its surroundings? No, not at all! It ignored its environment and just grew, being as beautiful as its Creator created it to be.

Without meaning to be rude, I yelled at my friend to stop so we could get out of the car. When she did, I ran to the tree. I wanted to see if it was as beautiful up close as it was when we were driving toward it. It was. Even more so!

I stood there, taking in its gloriousness. I knew I would take pictures, but I knew the pictures wouldn't do it justice. So, I just stood still, looking at it, trying to seal its beauty in my brain.

My friend told me the name of the tree is the flamboyant tree. And surely, it was bodacious, bold, brilliant, and breathtaking. It was the metaphor for my life: thriving in the midst of challenging circumstances.

INTRODUCTION

At the very outset of this work, I want to ask you a few questions. Are you a single mother now, or have you raised children by yourself? Have you been lied on, lied to, talked about, or mistreated, but you didn't lose your mind, didn't hurt anybody? Do you feel you have been knocked down by life—I mean flat on your face—so far down that even you doubted you would ever rise again? But you did, by the grace of God, get up. And you got up with attitude! "Yeah, that's right, I fell, but I'm back. Deal with it!"

If you answered yes to any or all of these questions, I would like for you to stop right now and applaud yourself! Celebrate yourself for not giving in, not giving up, and not throwing in the towel. You, my sisters, are the most beautiful, resilient creations on the planet. You have endured more, given more, sacrificed more, and had more expected of you than anyone else, and yet, you are the least appreciated and most undervalued. So, I celebrate you today!

There are so many traits I love about women: our sensitivity, our flexibility, our adaptability, our ability to bounce back after a devastating blow, our openness, our realness or authenticity, our ability to see and appreciate beauty even after being exposed to the brutal ugliness of life, our willingness to love, to give of ourselves in spite of numerous heartbreaks and disappointments, and our innate ability to identify and nurture the hurting. This trait is primal, instinctive, and reflexive. We can't help it!

And then, there is the African American woman who has the ability not just to survive but to *thrive*, to glow in the midst of the struggles, denials, and oppressions of life. There is a deeply rooted strength of the Black woman, borne out of centuries of mental, physical, and emotional abuse, rape, heartbreak, denial, loss, and other human tragedies. Yet, we emerge victorious. "How?" you may ask. We continue to love, give, encourage, give birth, teach, trust again, forgive, and hope. *We are hope, faith, and love!*

There is an awakening among women that we must do more for each other. How long has this been occurring? I'm not sure, but about twenty years ago, I became aware that God was calling me to do more to help women achieve their highest potential. However, in 2008, not too long after I accepted my call to preach the glorious gospel of Christ, I was cautioned by someone very close to me, someone whom I admire, trust, and respect a great deal, to be careful that I didn't find myself ministering to just women. I admit: his caution disturbed me greatly. So, I prayed and thought about what he had said. And the truth is this: I will minister to *anybody* and *everybody* who God sends my way. But the fact is *women in general, and minority women more specifically, need encouragement and uplifting,* and if I am privileged to do so, I will.

We women sometimes have to be convinced that there is greatness in us and that we are obligated to live out that greatness. We sometimes have to be convinced to allow God to manifest Himself in us so that our greatness will be realized. We women, as we grow and deal with the challenges of life, find ourselves in circumstances where we need a cheerleader telling us we can do it, we can make it. Well, I'm that cheerleader, and I believe God has called me to minister to all people but specifically to encourage and aid women to attain their highest potential. This is one aspect of my ministry. So, I will continue to tell women how wonderful they are.

The intent of this book is to inspire you toward your destiny by learning to thrive in the most challenging circumstances. It is a process that requires hope, courage, confidence, and knowing your purpose.

Why is hope important? Because people need hope! Hope is what gets us up in the morning and makes us keep trying to make it. Hope is that intangible essence that we can't see, touch, taste, or smell, but without it, we can't live. I don't know about you, but there have been times in my life when hope was all I had, and it was all I needed to keep going. I didn't have a clue. I didn't have a goal. I had no education. I didn't have any money. But I had hope. I will discuss hope more in Chapter 3.

Why are courage and confidence important? As an African American woman, I have struggled to emerge from the challenging circumstances in which I have often found myself. The struggle has required courage and confidence in order for me to move forward despite my mistakes, in spite of what others have said about me, and in spite of the attempt to place limitations on me. This struggle has produced a formidable personality, one that is often misunderstood. Seldom have I been congratulated or respected as a survivor. No matter. I am what I had to become to survive. It may not be pretty, and I am imperfect, but I am a work in progress. The resulting purpose is this: I am zealously pursuing excellence and am determined to thrive!

I define excellence as thriving in the midst of life's storms. Thriving is living in a manner that gives God glory in everything you do, whether it is creating a nurturing environment in your home for your spouse and children, performing your employment, operating in ministry, or building and fostering loving relationships. Thriving in the midst is required in everything!

This work, *In Christ, I Thrive (ICIT)*, was born out of an eight-year period of extreme challenges, disappointments, and failures in my life. It began as a single conference called The Pursuit of Excellence and initially addressed one aspect of my life: thriving in a challenging work environment. It has now expanded to this book and an annual conference called Thriving in the Midst.

ICIT begins with a discussion of Matthew 5:48 as it relates to perfection in Christ. I then discuss what it means "to thrive" based on my learning and experiences. I next address three areas of my life where I had to apply the principles revealed in the introduction of perfection. Those areas are: thriving in a challenging work environment, ministering in a tension-filled home, and women in leadership in ministry. Chapter 6 discusses abandonment. In the seventh chapter, I discuss how to engage in warfare when the enemy is attacking on more than one front at the same time. Chapter 8 discusses the supremacy of God's love for us. Chapter 9 discusses the importance of self-care, and Chapter 10 is the benediction.

At the end of each chapter are action items and a brief prayer. The action items are things for you to do, steps for you to take, practical application of the Word to your life that will facilitate your thriving.

I have to admit that, at various points throughout the writing of this book, I had doubts, not about the contents, but I wondered whether this work was really meant to be made public or was simply a therapeutic exercise for me. I soon discovered that, without a doubt, writing about how I dealt with the issues really helped me and caused me to remember past challenges and past victories. Also, not a week went by when I did not encounter some woman who expressed to me her challenges in one or several of the areas I talk about.

During my writing, I continually faced tests and trials in every area of my life.

As I neared the end of the writing, there were days I cried a lot because of "stuff" happening at home, at church, in the nonprofit organization where I volunteered, and in my family. Challenges and oppositions continued to confront me. As a result, I kept doing what I will tell you to do in this book, and there is great news: applying the principles kept me focused and kept bringing me back to a place of assurance in God's love and of who I am in Christ!

As godly women, we have to keep doing what the Holy Spirit has revealed will work. Keep the faith, read the Word, and do the work, and you will thrive in every challenging environment. Others will witness your walk and be blessed, and God will be glorified.

So, you have the book (praise the Lord), and I believe it will be a blessing to you as you read, focus, and commit to thriving to the glory of God!

thrive

Chapter 1

PERFECTION! REALLY? IN CHRIST!

When you are perfect in this sense, you lack nothing in your character; you are all that God created and destined you to be. When you are perfect, you are no longer broken. When you are perfect, you are at your best. When you become perfect, you have reached full maturity in Christ and become clothed in all that he is (Romans 13:14).

Dr. Cynthia Hale[1]

I am convinced that, in order to thrive, we must first understand the godly concept of perfection. In Matthew 5:48 (NKJV), Jesus tells us, "Therefore you shall be perfect just as your Father in heaven is perfect." This scripture has always intrigued and frightened me. How can I possibly be perfect with all my flaws, failures, and frailties? Nevertheless, I had to find a way to rectify this dilemma, knowing God would not tell me to do something I was not capable of doing.

The Greek word translated as "perfection" is *teleios*, which means "wholeness and completion." I believe that, as Christians, we can only realize our perfection (wholeness and completion) by realizing who we are *in Christ* and then embracing the *newness* that comes from receiving Christ as Savior. Let us look at what it means to be *in Christ*.

"Therefore, if anyone is in Christ, he is a new creation; old things have passed away; behold, all things have become new" (2 Corinthians 5:17, NKJV).

Beginning in November 2013 and continuing until February 2014, my personal Bible-study time consisted of an in-depth look at 1 and 2 Corinthians and the book of Romans.

Second Corinthians is addressed to the church in Corinth, advising them of Paul's impending visit. The primary theme of this epistle is that Christians demonstrate obedience to Christ by showing respect and submission to the authority of Christ's messenger. But as I studied 1 and 2 Corinthians, three other themes were strikingly evident to me in these letters: first, Paul's *authority*; second, Paul's *boldness*; and third, both his authority and boldness were rooted in his *newness*.

Throughout his writing, Paul uses the phrase "in Christ" in different ways. In one sense or understanding, when Paul writes "in Christ," he is referring to the sinner's conversion, the sinner's reception, the sinner's adoption, and the sinner's salvation being accomplished by what Christ did at the cross. Used in this sense, "in Christ" means "because of Christ" or "through Christ," as used in Romans 6:23 (KJV): "For the wages of sin is death; but the gift of God is eternal life in [through] Jesus Christ our Lord" (hereinafter, comments in brackets mine).

There was only one acceptable sacrifice for our sin that God would receive; that was the unblemished righteousness of Christ. As a result of Christ offering Himself on the cross as the perfect sacrifice, His righteousness is imputed to all who will believe in Him and the finished work of the cross.

You can find other instances of "in Christ" used in this sense in the following scriptures: Romans 6:11, 8:39, 12:5, 15:17, 16:3, 16:7, 16:9; 1 Corinthians 1:2, 1:30, 4:10, 4:15, 4:17, 15:31, 16:24; 2 Corinthians 1:21, 2:14, 3:14, 11:3, 12:2; Galatians 1:22, 2:4, 3:14, 3:17, 3:26, 3:28, 5:6; Ephesians 1:1, 1:3, 1:10, 1:20, 2:6, 2:7, 2:10,

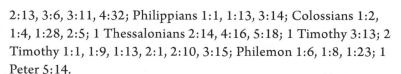

2:13, 3:6, 3:11, 4:32; Philippians 1:1, 1:13, 3:14; Colossians 1:2, 1:4, 1:28, 2:5; 1 Thessalonians 2:14, 4:16, 5:18; 1 Timothy 3:13; 2 Timothy 1:1, 1:9, 1:13, 2:1, 2:10, 3:15; Philemon 1:6, 1:8, 1:23; 1 Peter 5:14.

The other sense in which Paul uses the phrase "in Christ" means "walking after the Spirit" or "living according to the direction of the Holy Spirit." In this sense, to be "in Christ" means that your spirit, soul, and body have come into alignment and agreement with the Spirit of God in you. An example of this usage is in Romans 8:1 (NKJV): "There is therefore now no condemnation to those who are in Christ Jesus, who do not walk according to the flesh, but according to the Spirit." "In Christ" in this verse means to desire and pursue the things of God, to live a life yielded to the control of God's Spirit and not the self-seeking, self-centered, sinful dictates of one's desires.

"Walking in the Spirit" describes a life yielded to the control of God's Spirit, a life that enthusiastically accepts and gratefully embraces the grace of God and seeks to be lived in a manner that does not exploit or take His grace for granted. This yielding to the Spirit produces the fruit of the Spirit, as stated in Galatians 5:22–23, which are love, joy, peace, long-suffering, kindness, goodness, faithfulness, gentleness, and self-control.

Often, it is difficult to walk in the Spirit because, as Matthew 26:41 (NKJV) tells us, we have to "watch and pray, lest you enter into temptation. The spirit indeed is willing, but the flesh is weak." So how do we begin this transformation of coming into alignment, of walking in the Spirit, walking *in Christ?*

It starts with your mind. That is why the Word of God tells us in Romans 12:2 (NKJV), "Do not be conformed to this world, but be transformed by the renewing of your mind, that you may prove what is that good and acceptable and perfect will of God."

How do you renew your mind? By reading, studying, and meditating on the Word of God. The Word of God is relevant and life-changing. The Word of God edifies. It is our road map for life (here and now and eternally). The Word satisfies the desires and emptiness of our soul, which is our intellect, will, and emotions. The Word nourishes

17

every aspect of our being. The Word feeds us. It is indeed the *bread of heaven* (John 6:22–51). The Word draws us to God and propels us toward our destiny. The Word speaks to the challenges of life. It lacks nothing.

> The word of God is living and powerful, and sharper than any two-edged sword, piercing even to the division of soul and spirit, and of joints and marrow, and is a discerner of the thoughts and intents of the heart.
>
> Hebrews 4:12 (NKJV)

This means the Word of God is able to get deep into our souls and spirits, identifying what we ought to be and what we can be only in Christ. The Word of God reveals to us the Holy Spirit and His ability to empower us to be like Christ.

How do you renew your mind? You do so by being purposeful in what you allow and receive into your mind, by being purposeful in what you read and listen to, purposeful in what you believe and what you meditate on.

Philippians 4:8 (NKJV) tells us to meditate on

> whatever things are true, whatever things are noble, whatever things are just, whatever things are pure, whatever things are lovely, whatever things are of good report, if there is any virtue and if there is anything praiseworthy— meditate on these things.

Meditating on these things initiates the renewing of your mind, and the best source for what is true and noble and pure and of good report and praiseworthy is the Word of God.

Listening to, reading, and studying the Word of God leads to right believing and right thinking, and right thinking leads to right living, or, in other words, walking in the Spirit.

We cannot see ourselves as new until we see ourselves *in Christ*. We cannot really understand what that means until we read and study the Word and allow the Holy Spirit to illuminate and give understanding. When He does this, our minds come into agreement with Him.

Philippians 2:5–7 (NKJV) says,

> Let this mind be in you which was also in Christ Jesus, who, being in the form of God, did not consider it robbery to be equal with God but made Himself of no reputation, taking the form of a bondservant, and coming in the likeness of men.

What was the mind that was in Christ Jesus? Knowing He was equal to God and a coparticipant with God the Father and God the Holy Spirit, instead of asserting His right as a member of the Trinity, our Lord waived His rights and humbled Himself. Christ had a mind of service and humility. How did Christ think? He chose to serve and to save. What did He believe in? He believed in His Father. What did He place His faith in? He had faith in who He was in the Father.

This is the mind we must have to be *in Christ*, placing our trust and faith in Him, who He is, what He has done for us, and His amazing grace.

In our own strength, in our own reasoning, in our own thinking, and in our own understanding, we can do nothing but fail. That is why the Word of God tells us in Proverbs 3:5–6 (NKJV), "Trust in the Lord with all your heart, and lean not on your own understanding; in all your ways acknowledge Him, and He shall direct your paths."

As your mind, your thinking, begins to come into alignment with the Spirit of God living within you, your body, your physical being, your flesh, has to be dealt with, as it too struggles with the newness of you.

Your body is the temple where the Spirit of the living God dwells, but the flesh is crazy. That is why in Romans 7, Paul talks about the war within himself. He writes, "For I know that in me (that is, in my flesh) nothing good dwells" (Romans 7:18, NKJV). Paul talks about evil being present with him at all times even though he delighted in doing the will of God.

Paul was so frustrated that he said of himself, "O wretched man that I am!" He cried out in anguish this QUESTION: "Who will deliver me from this body of death?" And then he had an "aha" moment when the Holy Spirit reminded him who had delivered him: "Jesus Christ our Lord!" (Romans 7:24–25, NKJV).

Once Paul walked *in Christ*, he yielded his life to the control of God's Spirit. Again, yielding to the Spirit produces the fruit of the Spirit, which is the evidence of your perfection (wholeness and completion).

"In Christ" according to Ephesians 1:2–14 (NKJV):

> Grace to you and peace from God our Father and the Lord Jesus Christ. Blessed be the God and Father of our Lord Jesus Christ, who has blessed us with every spiritual blessing in the heavenly places in Christ, just as He chose us in Him before the foundation of the world, that we should be holy and without blame before Him in love, having predestined us to adoption as sons by Jesus Christ to Himself, according to the good pleasure of His will, to the praise of the glory of His grace, by which He made us accepted in the Beloved. In Him we have redemption through His blood, the forgiveness of sins, according to the riches of His grace which He made to abound toward us in all wisdom and prudence, having made known to us the mystery of His will, according to His good pleasure which He purposed in Himself, that in the dispensation of the fullness of the times He might gather together in one all things in Christ, both which are in heaven and which are on earth—in Him. In Him also we have obtained an inheritance, being predestined according to the purpose of Him who works all things according to the counsel of His will, that we who first trusted in Christ should be to the praise of His glory. In Him you also trusted, after you heard the word

of truth, the gospel of your salvation; in whom also, having believed, you were sealed with the Holy Spirit of promise, who is the guarantee of our inheritance until the redemption of the purchased possession, to the praise of His glory.

In most of Paul's writing to specific people or churches, he writes to address specific problems or correct errors of false teaching. But in his letter to the church in Ephesus, Paul identifies spiritual assets that we, believers, have received as a result of accepting Christ so that we might fulfill God's overall purpose for the church, which is to bring praise and glory to God. Ephesians, chapter 1, verses 2–14, points out very specific assets, attributes, blessings received as a result of the work Christ accomplished on the cross:

In Christ, we are the recipients of grace and peace.

"Grace to you and peace from God our Father and the Lord Jesus Christ" (verse 2).

"Grace" and "peace" are a reminder of the finished work of the cross. Grace has always been given to us, even when we were still in our sins. That's why we had chance after chance to receive Christ as Savior—because of grace. What is grace? I looked up the Greek definition of "grace" and researched other theologically respected resources for a definition, and the definitions vary depending on the context in which the word is used. But when the word "grace" is used predicated of Yahweh (God, our Lord), it indicates the unconditional, unmerited, and unearned granting of His blessing. *Grace* is receiving the goodness and blessings of God that we did not deserve.

What is peace? The Greek word defines "peace" as "prosperity," "quietness," "rest," and "set at one again" (restored). We can only have peace by accepting Jesus Christ and believing in the work He accomplished on the cross.

In Christ, we are blessed with every spiritual blessing.

"Blessed be the God and Father of our Lord Jesus Christ, who has blessed us with every spiritual blessing in the heavenly places in Christ" (verse 3).

Every spiritual blessing is the inheritance we receive in Christ, every benefit of the atonement. Atonement is the reconciliation between God and man based on Christ paying the price for our sins on the cross. Some specific blessings are forgiveness of sins, eternal life with God, righteousness, joy, and peace in the Holy Spirit. We are blessed and freely given these benefits when we are in Christ.

In Christ, we are chosen, holy, and blameless.

"[…] just as He chose us in Him before the foundation of the world, that we should be holy and without blame before Him in love" (verse 4).

God decided He would choose those and receive those who accepted Jesus as Savior because Jesus paid the price for our sins. God also decided that, as a result of accepting Christ as Savior, we would be holy and blameless in Christ.

In Christ, we are predestined and adopted.

"[…] having predestined us to adoption as sons by Jesus Christ to Himself, according to the good pleasure of His will […]" (verse 5).

God preordained, predetermined, and decided before the foundation of the world was laid that those who believed in Christ and the completed work of the cross would be adopted as joint heirs with Christ. We would be legally received when we accept Christ as Savior as the only means to this adoption.

In Christ, we are the praise of the glory of His grace.

"[…] to the praise of the glory of His grace, by which He made us accepted in the Beloved" (verse 6).

He accepts us into His glory because of what Christ did. When we are in Christ, we highlight the grace, goodness, glory, and majesty of God. We magnify His glory. We call attention to His glory. When we are in Christ, we shine in Him! When we are in Christ, our existence and presence make a boast of His greatness. We brag on Him!

In Christ, we have redemption and forgiveness.

"In Him [Jesus] we have redemption through His blood, the forgiveness of sins, according to the riches of His grace" (verse 7).

When we are in Christ, we are released from the bondage of our sins. Christ's substitutionary death fully satisfied God's justice. And we are restored since sin no longer creates a barrier between God and us. Our debt to God has been paid by Christ, and therefore, we are forgiven of the indebtedness.

In Christ, we are wise, prudent, and given revelation.

[…] which He made to abound toward us in all wisdom and prudence, having made known to us the mystery of His will, according to His good pleasure which He purposed in Himself, that in the dispensation of the fullness of the times He might gather together in one all things in Christ, both which are in heaven and which are on earth—in Him.

Verses 8–10

God's grace, which is given to us freely and in unlimited proportion, allows the Holy Spirit to help us understand, to a degree, the "mystery" of the gospel; that is, the doctrine and principles, Christian dispensation and the secret purposes and counsel God intends to carry out in His kingdom. We are not made to understand it all, but we are allowed to understand to a degree with the help of the Holy Spirit. And in the fullness of time or the summing up of all things in Christ, both in heaven and on the earth, Christ will take charge. And as our elders used to say, "We'll understand it better by and by."

This knowledge given to us allows us to be informed, enlightened, wise, and prudent, offering us the ability to govern and discipline ourselves by the use of reason and the leading of the Holy Spirit.

In Christ, we are legitimate.

"In Him also we have obtained an inheritance, being predestined according to the purpose of Him who works all things according to the counsel of His will" (verse 11).

What is an inheritance? According to Merriam-Webster's Dictionary, inheritance is defined in part as

- "The reception of genetic qualities by transmission from parent to offspring."

- "The acquisition of a possession, condition, or trait from past generations."[2]

- Usually, something of value.

- Inheritance speaks to legitimacy. You can only inherit what has been designated to you by someone else who decides to identify you as their heir and, thus, wants to bequeath to you something the giver deems valuable. When the giver identifies one as the recipient of an inheritance, it indicates that the giver "owns" or receives or embraces you as his or her legitimate heir.

The giver may impose certain conditions that have to be met by the heir before the heir can receive the inheritance.

Because of sin, we were separated from our Father, disconnected due to the corruption of man. We were cut off from our Father. The condition that God the Father decided had to be met for our restoration to Him was an unblemished, perfect sacrifice. And God the Son, Jesus Christ, was the only being who could meet the condition by giving His life on the cross. Once He did so, mankind was eligible for full restoration and legitimacy. His sacrifice restored the full benefits of kinship available to us when we believe in and accept that finished work.

The inheritance of salvation we receive in Christ gives us legitimacy. This makes us God's heritage, His legacy, His heirs (when we accept the work of the cross), and thus, we have all the heavenly privileges that Christ has. And so, we are made legitimate and "richer" because of being in Christ.

In Christ, we are the praise of His glory.

"[…] that we who first trusted in Christ should be to the praise of His glory" (verse 12).

When we are in Christ, we highlight God's glory and His saving grace to the world. We are the evidence of His glory when we are in Christ!

In Christ, we are wise and sealed.

In Him you also trusted, after you heard the word of truth, the gospel of your salvation; in whom also, having believed, you were sealed with the Holy Spirit of promise, who is the guarantee of our inheritance until the redemption of the purchased possession, to the praise of His glory.

Verses 13–14

We were wise to trust when we heard the truth of the saving power of the cross. The sealing is the Holy Spirit's presence in our lives. When we are in Christ, we are kept or guided from doing ungodly things, we are assured of the finished work of the cross; we are preserved for eternity, we are guaranteed a place in heaven as a joint heir with Christ, we are counseled as to how to live in the righteousness given to us by Jesus's work on the cross, and we are protected from and helped to overcome the tricks of the devil—all because of the Holy Spirit living in us!

I think now would be a good time to remind you of all the spiritual blessings we receive when we are in Christ. We are:

- recipients of grace and peace,
- blessed,
- chosen,
- holy,
- blameless,
- predestined,
- adopted,
- accepted,
- redeemed,

- forgiven,

- informed,

- enlightened,

- given revelation,

- legitimate,

- recipients of an inheritance (legacy),

- praise of His glory,

- wise,

- sealed.

New Creation

Hopefully, you now have a better understanding of what Paul meant when he wrote of us being "new creations." I don't know about you, but when I consider the above list of attributes and benefits ascribed to me after receiving Christ as Savior, I can see I look nothing like the person I used to be. Praise the Lord! I am far from perfect in my human efforts and strength, but I rest in the secure knowledge of what Christ accomplished on the cross. Because of what He did and my believing and receiving it, I can also believe I am everything God says I am, not because of my efforts, but because I am in Christ.

Newness in Christ facilitates perfection (wholeness and completion). Embracing this newness is evidence that you are no longer burdened by your past. You are, instead, living in the fullness of God's love and appreciating the benefits of His grace.

Let us continue to examine the teachings and life of the apostle Paul to get a better understanding of newness and perfection.

Paul's newness in Christ was the basis on which he staked every-thing he did. Paul was not bound by his past; he was not troubled by who or what he used to be. How can I tell? Let's look a little closer at 2 Corinthians 5:14 (NKJV): "For the love of Christ compels us because we judge thus: that if One died for all, then all died." Verse 15 tells us why Paul reached the conclusion he did: "And He died for all that those who live should live no longer for themselves, but for Him who died for them and rose again."

In this text, we are reminded of the love of Christ, demonstrated by what Christ did for us on the cross. We are reminded of His supreme sacrifice. It is the love of Christ, the sacrifice of Christ, and our acceptance of His sacrifice that enable us to achieve perfection.

We have been saved by the blood, and what we were before salvation has been done away with because of what Christ accom-plished on the cross. God restored us back to Himself and has not held mankind responsible for sin. Instead, the penalty of sin was imputed to, assigned to, ascribed to, and placed on Christ. He paid the price for us!

Paul was confident in the completed work accomplished by Christ at the cross, and because of that, Paul had a blessed assurance that he was new.

Yet, in spite of his newness, Paul had his thorn, his issue, something powerful that constantly tested and challenged his newness. But once Paul relied upon the sufficient grace of God and not his own strength, he boldly declared in 1 Corinthians 4:16 (NKJV), "Therefore I urge you, *imitate me*" (hereinafter, emphasis mine). He said it again in 1 Corinthians 11:1 (NKJV), "*Imitate me*, just as I also imitate Christ."

Paul was saying that when you don't know what to do, ask yourself, "What would Paul do?" and then do that because Paul was doing what Christ would have done.

Now, Paul didn't deny his past—to the contrary. In 1 Corinthians 16:9 (NKJV), Paul says, "For I am the least of the apostles, who am not worthy to be called an apostle, because I persecuted the church of God." Paul knew what he deserved—*death*. But Paul also knew what he had received because of grace. He had received newness and eternal life.

Paul knew and boldly affirmed in 2 Corinthians 3:4–5 (NKJV), "And we have such trust through Christ toward God. Not that we are sufficient of ourselves to think of anything as being from ourselves, but our sufficiency is from God."

Paul made it clear in 2 Corinthians 4:5 that he preached not himself but Christ Jesus the Lord and that he was qualified, certified, justified, and sanctified to preach this glorious gospel.

Paul knew and asserted in 2 Corinthians 5:17 (NKJV), "Therefore, if anyone is in Christ, he is a new creation; old things have passed away; behold, all things have become new."

He was a completely new being with new thinking and new living, and it was all dependent solely on the grace of God.

God is always calling us, directing us to forget the old stuff and see the newness, the new beginnings of our lives, and the newness of our situations if we are *in Christ*.

However, this principle of newness did not originate with Paul. In Isaiah 43:18–19, the Lord tells us, through the prophet Isaiah, to forget the former things. They are nothing compared to what He is doing now and will do in our future.

Lamentations 3:23, widely believed to have been authored by the prophet Jeremiah, tells us we have *new* mercies.

In Romans 6:4 (NKJV), Paul tells us, "Therefore, we were buried with him through baptism into death, that just as Christ was raised from the dead by the glory of the Father, even so we also should walk in the *newness* of life."

Paul completely embraced his newness *in Christ* with no reservations. He looked back over his life on more than one occasion and was brutally honest about how he had ardently and enthusiastically persecuted the church. When he was that person, Saul, he did his job with great vigor and passion. He gave it his all—no holding back. But when he met Christ, all things changed!

Yes, Paul understood and embraced his newness. Likewise, he understood, embraced, and depended on the grace of God.

In Ephesians 2:1–3 (NKJV), Paul writes,

> He made us alive, who were dead in trespasses and sins, in which you once walked according to the course of this world, according to the prince of the power of the air, the spirit who now works in the sons of disobedience, among whom also we all once conducted ourselves in the lusts of our flesh, fulfilling the desires of the flesh and of the mind, and were by nature children of wrath, just as the others.

In other words, mankind walked in total depravity because of sin. How could Paul be so convinced of his newness? Verses 4 through 10 of Ephesians 2 describe what made Paul so sure.

> *But God who is rich in mercy, because of His great love with which He loved us, even when we were dead in trespasses, in sin, God made us alive together with Christ (by grace you have been saved), and raised us up together, and made us sit together in the heavenly places in Christ Jesus, that in the ages to come He might show the exceeding riches of His grace in His kindness toward us in Christ Jesus. For by grace you have been saved through faith, and that not of yourselves; it is the gift of God, not of works, lest anyone should boast. For we are His workmanship, created in Christ Jesus for good works, which God prepared beforehand that we should walk in them.*

Verse 4 of Ephesians 2 begins with an emphatic, unequivocal declaration: "But God"! Often, when you find in the Scripture these two words, "but God," coming together, regardless of what happened before, this conjunction, "but," causes you to stop, take a deep breath, make a reassessment, and prepare yourself for the good news that is ahead. This conjunction, "but," attached to the name of the sovereign God, changes everything.

Please consider the following references:

- In Genesis 31:7 (NKJV), Jacob said to Rachel and Leah about Laban, "Yet your father has deceived me and changed my wages ten times, *but God* did not allow him to hurt me."

- In Genesis 50:20 (NKJV), Joseph said to his brothers, "But as for you, you meant evil against me; *but God* meant it for good, in order to bring it about as it is this day, to save many people alive."

- In 1 Samuel 23:14 (NKJV), "And David stayed in strongholds in the wilderness, and remained in the mountains in the Wilderness of Ziph. Saul sought him every day, *but God* did not deliver him into his hand."

- In Psalm 73:26 (NKJV), the psalmist said, "My flesh and my heart fail; *But God* is the strength of my heart and my portion forever."

- In 1 Corinthians 10:13 (NKJV), Paul said,

  No temptation has overtaken you except such as is common to man; *but God is faithful, who will not allow you to be tempted beyond what you are able, but with the temptation will also make the way of escape, that you may be able to bear it.*

Allow me to utilize the twenty-first-century vernacular. How many of you can attest today that you should have been, would have been, could have been dead, *but God?* You could have had AIDS, *but God!* You have been lied on, *but God!* Friends walked away with no explanation, *but God!* You have been left alone, *but God!* You have been misunderstood, *but God!* You were guilty, *but God!* You drank it, smoked it, snorted it, *but God!* You cheated, *but God!* You mistreated somebody, *but God!* You have been confused, *but God!* Maybe you have been abused and molested, *but God!*

"But God" changes everything. It is on this principle that Paul staked his life, his ministry, and the lives of all those to whom he preached. Paul had a blessed assurance in this grace of God. Paul knew that the same grace that facilitated his salvation and brought about his newness would keep him, sustain him, protect him, deliver him, and enable him to attain perfection (wholeness and completion).

There are many uncertainties in life, but there are some things I have a blessed assurance about based on the Word of God.

Isaiah 54:17: I am convinced that no weapon formed against me shall prosper and that every tongue that rises against me in judgment I shall condemn. Why? Because this is my heritage as a servant of the Lord.

John 3:16: I know that God so loved the world that He gave His only begotten Son, that whoever believes in Him should not perish but have everlasting life.

Romans 8:35–39: I am convinced that even as I face tribulation, distress, persecution, or peril, in all these things, I am more than a conqueror through Him who loves me. I am persuaded that neither death nor life, nor angels, nor principalities, nor powers, nor things present, nor things to come, nor height, nor depth, nor any other created thing shall be able to separate me from the love of God, which is in Christ Jesus our Lord.

Philippians 1:6: I am confident of this very thing: that He who has begun a good work in me will complete it until the day of Jesus Christ.

Anyone can have this same assurance. Having been saved by accepting the power of Christ, which was demonstrated by His death, resurrection, and ascension, we now have certain protection from and authority over the enemy, and he knows this.

Now the enemy will try to fool you, inconvenience you, and trick you into believing otherwise, but if you are God's property, paid for with the blood of Jesus, and if you accept His authority over your life, the Holy Spirit is going to empower you to completely conquer the enemy, embrace your newness, and become whole and complete (perfect) in Him.

Becoming whole and complete is a process. It is a journey, but when you are in Christ, you are equipped for the journey because of the Holy Spirit living inside of you. Reconcile your mind and be okay with the fact that it is a process and you will experience setbacks. Don't get frustrated. Don't be fooled by the enemy that you are not doing it right. When you have accepted Christ as Savior, you can do all things through Him because, by His Holy Spirit, you are strengthened.

Each trial brings a greater degree of newness. Each test takes you to another level of understanding. Each persecution produces a greater level of patience. Each tribulation better defines your character. And each struggle brings a greater revelation of who Jesus is and who you are in Him. This is one understanding of going "from glory to glory" (2 Corinthians 3:16–18). As you go through every trial, test, persecution, tribulation, and struggle by applying the Word of God, the Holy Spirit transforms you into the image of God from glory to ever-increasing glory. And as you go from glory to glory, you come into a new way of knowing that is not based on the external or the carnal, fleshly knowledge. The new way of knowing is based on the spiritual assessment of the new nature that is given to you through Christ.

When you receive the saving grace of Christ, you are a new creation, old things have passed away; "forgetting those things which are behind" (Philippians 3:13, NKJV), behold, you have become new.

As Christians, some of us are not experiencing all that God has for us because the enemy has us so rooted and bogged down in our past. But once we engage new thinking and new believing, once we initiate new living with the help and direction of the Holy Spirit, and once we dare to believe God and dream new dreams based on His plan for our lives, we walk into a new *destiny,* a *new purpose,* and a *blessed assurance* that by His grace we are what we are, transformed and new.

What does this newness look like? Colossians 3:12–17 (NKJV) tells us,

Therefore, as the elect of God, holy and beloved, put on tender mercies, kindness, humility, meekness, long-suffering; bearing with one another, and forgiving one another, if anyone has a complaint against another; even as Christ forgave you, so you also must do. But above all these things put on love, which is the bond of perfection. And let the peace of God rule in your hearts, to which also you were called in one body; and be thankful. Let the word of Christ dwell in you richly in all wisdom, teaching and admonishing one another in psalms and hymns and spiritual songs, singing with grace in your hearts to the Lord. And whatever you do in word or deed, do all in the name of the Lord Jesus, giving thanks to God the Father through Him.

This is the portrait of newness. This is also the portrait of perfection.

What is keeping you from embracing your newness today? Is it fear, fear of failure, fear of what others will think, fear that maybe your newness isn't really real?

If you have accepted Christ as Savior, you've been bathed in the blood of Jesus. You have been cleansed from all your sins, and you are a new creation.

In Matthew 5:48, when Christ speaks of perfection, He is teaching us that our imitation of our heavenly Father must be an earnest and continuous effort. The Holy Spirit alone can help us accomplish this pursuit, which He does according to our faith in Christ and the finished work on the cross (Romans 8:1–2, 11).

It is in our newness in Christ that we realize perfection (wholeness and completion), and it is this realization of who we are in Him that causes us to thrive in all areas of our lives. Pursuing excellence brings us closer to God, and getting closer to God brings excellence and perfection (wholeness and completion). It is a glorious cycle, a high calling of God, which is in Christ Jesus (Philippians 3:12–14). This is *thriving*, and it is my earnest prayer that this book will aid you in doing so. I have endeavored to make it a practical, everyday approach with things to do and not to do in order to strive for this high calling of thriving in the midst!

Action Items: Meditation

For the next week, meditate accordingly:

- Monday: focus on God Himself.

- Tuesday: focus on His Word.

- Wednesday: focus on His works/creation.

- Thursday: focus on past victories where you overcame the enemy's tricks.

- Friday: focus on positive thoughts of who you are in Christ according to Ephesians 1:2–14.

- Saturday: focus on the promises of God.

- Sunday: focus on His Word (again).

Choose two or three short scriptural passages that refer to the topic of the day and read or recite them several times during the day or make your own positive, affirming thought about the topic for the day. For example, on Monday, you could recite Genesis 1:1 (NKJV), "In the beginning God created the heavens and the earth," or some of the names of God, such as El-Hanam, "God is gracious"; El-Shaddai, "God is almighty"; El-Elyon, "the Most High," "the exalted One"; El-Olam, "the everlasting One"; El-Berith, "God of the covenant"; El-Roi. "God who sees me"; Elohim, "Infinite." Record any revelation, new thinking, or additional scriptures that the Holy Spirit gives you.

Affirmation

- Begin to identify specific scriptures that speak to who you are in Christ. You can refer to the scriptures I listed at the beginning of this chapter or look for others. Learn them and memorize them, but until you do, write them down in a notebook or electronic device (phone or tablet) for quick access for times when you need to encourage yourself.

The following are some of my favorite affirming scriptures:

- 1 Corinthians 1:30

- Philippians 1:6

- Isaiah 54:13–15

Prayer

Father God, thank You that we do not have to depend on our own efforts to achieve perfection. It is only through what Christ did on the cross that perfection (wholeness and completion) is possible. Holy Spirit, teach us to lean and depend on the finished work at the cross. In Jesus's name, we pray. Amen.

Reflections

_____
_____
_____
_____
_____
_____
_____
_____
_____
_____
_____
_____
_____
_____
_____
_____
_____
_____
_____
_____
_____
_____

thrive

Chapter 2

THE CONCEPT OF THRIVING

The thief does not come except to steal, and to kill, and to destroy. I have come that they may have life, and that they may have it more abundantly.

John 10:10 (NKJV)

What do you think of when you hear or see the words "abundant," "thriving," "flourish," or "overflow"? For me, these words evoke feelings of security and happiness and speak of possibilities. With the fact that God uses these words to tell us what we can expect when we are in Christ, one might believe that there would be no challenges in our lives. But the Bible also tells us that when we are in Christ, we can expect trials (James 1:2), tribulations (Romans 12:12), and afflictions (Psalm 34:19). How do we reconcile both truths? We must learn to live according to the Word of God in order to thrive and live above mediocre circumstances in spite of challenges.

In John 10:10, Jesus gives us a dire warning when He tells us that Satan's purpose is "to steal, and to kill, and to destroy." However, His next few words bring great joy! He assures us that through Him, we can have life and "have *it* more abundantly." To do so, we must understand what it means "to be in Christ." That is why I began this work with the discussion in Chapter 1.

I pray that your understanding of who you are in Christ will be ongoing. This knowledge will continue to be the foundation for your life. Now I want to discuss *thriving*.

"To thrive" means "to grow vigorously," "to gain in wealth or possessions," "to progress toward or realize a goal despite or because of circumstances."[3] One thing I discovered is that my understanding of what it means "to thrive" has grown and changed as I have learned more about who I am in Christ. I thought it would be helpful to describe the different levels of thriving that I encountered in my life. I want to stress that each person's definition or understanding of *thriving* will be specific to their walk of faith. However, the following is a basic understanding of *thriving* at different levels.

The Concept of Thriving

I have identified three levels of thriving. They are the *faith level*, the *abundant level*, and the *overflow level*. At each level of thriving, there were identifiable characteristics present in my life.

Faith Level

At the faith level, the following characteristics were present:

- When confronted with challenges, I could declare, "I'm still in my right mind." How did I know? Because I still trusted God.

- Consistent prayer was difficult for me, but I understood it to be essential to my walk with the Lord.

- I believed the Word despite no visible evidence that it was working.

- I believed what the Word said about me.

- I knew who I was in Christ (at least I had a beginning knowledge).

- I ministered to others, despite my challenges.

- I mentored others when the opportunity presented itself.

This is faith-level thriving.

Abundant Level

At the abundant level of thriving, the following characteristics were present:

- All of the above at the faith level and:

- I became more spiritually sound in my understanding and was no longer easily shaken by my challenges.

- There was evidence of my walk in the Lord; my attitude, presence, and demeanor reflected the *love of God!*

- My prayer life consisted of daily, focused prayer, and I looked forward to my quiet time with the Lord. It no longer felt like a duty, and I understood prayer to be a privilege.

- This is abundant-level thriving.

Overflow Level

At the overflow level of thriving, the following characteristics were present:

- All of the characteristics in the faith and abundant levels, as well as:

- I have consistent, direct impact on the lives of others spiritually, personally, and financially.

- I am able to meet the needs of others, and I delight in doing so.

- I engage in focused prayer two to three times daily.

- I regularly fast (for myself and others as the need arises and the Holy Spirit directs).

- I have a set time of consecration.

At each level of thriving, I asked the Holy Spirit to help me clearly see where I was and how I could do better. Consistently, new knowledge and understanding of who I am in Christ ushered me into deeper insight into what it means "to thrive." As you grow in the knowledge of who you are in Christ, your understanding of thriving will emerge. I pray this will be as fulfilling for you as it has been for me.

Action Item

Begin writing down what it means to you "to thrive." Don't worry about a precise definition at this point. It will probably evolve in the weeks ahead.

Prayer

Gracious Father, thank You for the promise of abundant life through Jesus Christ. Holy Spirit, please help me know how to live the fullest life I am intended to have because of Christ's sacrifice on the cross. In His name, I pray. Amen!

Reflections

_____

_____

_____

_____

_____

_____

_____

_____

_____

_____

_____

_____

_____

_____

_____

_____

_____

_____

_____

_____

thrive

Chapter 3

THRIVING IN A CHALLENGING WORK ENVIRONMENT

And whatever you do, do it heartily, as to the Lord and not to men, knowing that from the Lord you will receive the reward of the inheritance; for you serve the Lord Christ.

Colossians 3:23–24 (NKJV)

*N*ow that we understand that perfection (wholeness and completion) is available and achievable only in Christ, we are positioned to thrive as we encounter the challenges of life.

Thriving is being your best "you" in Christ, whole and complete, despite what may be said about you or done to you. Pursuing excellence is being consistently conscientious, diligent, trustworthy, a person of integrity, and subjected to those in authority (Titus 2:9–3:1). Pursuing excellence is doing your best at all times even if, and especially if, you do not think you are being treated right.

Thriving is continuing to love and forgive and grow in the things of God, even in the most uncomfortable, negative environment. Thriving is not falling apart when everything and everyone else around you are succumbing to the challenges. Knowing your strength comes from the Lord, you display a controlled, serene, confident demeanor. You demonstrate *grace* under fire; that is the grace of God working in your life. *Thriving in the midst of all situations is striving for this state of certainty in Christ.*

The workplace is one of the most common arenas in which the enemy of believers attacks. Statistics have proven time and time again that women in the workplace continue to be paid less than their male counterparts, and African American and Hispanic women are paid less than their white colleagues.[4] It is not our imagination that we face workplace and gender inequalities daily. When we are vocal in our opposition to these inequities, we are often branded as angry, militant, radical, difficult to work with, and other disrespectful labels. These labels act as chains that bind us to prevent us from reaching our full potential.

I encourage you, I beseech you, I implore you to push past the labels and walk into your destiny. Do not allow society to use these labels as negative barriers to hold you back. And don't you dare allow yourself to use these labels as excuses to live out a mundane life! You can't control what they say about you, but you can control what you think and say about yourself. You must choose positive, creative, empowering labels for yourself, such as "smart," "beautiful," "healthy," "honorable," and "anointed."

Another challenge that some women face is working in male-dominated professions and often finding themselves to be the "only one": the *only* woman and/or the *only* Black or Hispanic woman. Because of this challenge, we sometimes find ourselves doing some strange things, such as thinking we have to take less than what we deserve or that we must compromise or adjust who we are to be accepted as part of the mainstream. This creates tension within oneself. This creates an environment of anxiety within oneself.

Whether the challenges in the work environment are less pay, unfair criticism, harassment of any type, or being the only woman present, these antagonistic conditions can have devastating consequences, both professionally and personally. The most common consequences: the woman becomes cynical, too aggressive, too passive, or fearful. This book and the Thriving in the Midst (TITM) conference are designed to help women overcome these conditions, live up to their fullest professional, personal, and spiritual potential, and not lose themselves in the process.

TITM emerged out of my more than thirty-three years in law enforcement. During my employment time, I witnessed women who were angry, depressed, argumentative, fearful, and passive, all because of their work environment, and I said I would never let that happen to me. But sometime in 2001, I realized I was falling into that same trap of self-pity, pessimism, and anger because of what was or was not happening at work. My work performance never suffered. On the contrary, I excelled in performing my duties in whatever assignment I was placed. But I was becoming someone inside who I did not like at all. When I realized this, I immediately knew I had to do something. I began to pray and ask God for guidance, and over a period of just a few months, my attitude and my heart began to change. When I utilized the Word of God and other resources I found, the Holy Spirit began to change me from the inside out. Apparently, it showed because coworkers began to seek me out and ask for direction and guidance. I began to "counsel" people, either one-on-one or in small groups of two or three. I was able to have a direct impact on my work environment. I was amazed!

In 2005, a group of women from a local church asked me to speak to them about Christian women in the workplace. They felt that, because of the level of "success" I had achieved, I had valuable information that would be helpful to them. Again, I was amazed, but I began to actually write something down. This was when Thriving in the Midst developed into a formal presentation. It is the actual "formula" I used to revive myself. Since 2005, I have presented it to both Christian and professional organizations. It is developed from a Christian perspective, and its target audience is women. However, the principles apply regardless of your gender or your religious beliefs.

Success

I began this work by emphasizing that you should know who you are in Christ and the concept of what it means "to thrive." Let's continue with a definition of "success." The *Merriam-Webster Collegiate Dictionary* defines success as "a favorable or desired outcome; also: the attainment of wealth, favor, or eminence."[5]

Allen's Definition of Success

When I considered what success meant to me, I determined that true success means becoming the person God has called me to be and reaching the destiny He has set for my life. As this relates to work, success is:

- To come to work every day with an attitude of pursuing excellence, which is doing the very best I can, every time, with what I have to work with.

- To foster an atmosphere of excellence without micromanaging.

- To be effective and productive in the work environment.

- Not to be adversely affected by external circumstances.

- Learning something new every day.

- Encouraging and helping others to strive for their highest potential in all areas of their life.

- To keep hope alive, no matter what.

My success is not to any degree dependent on what others think of me but completely on what I know about myself and who I am in Christ. Success is knowing who I am and not being adversely affected on the inside by outside circumstances.

However you define success, there are things you will need to know and do to be successful, especially in a challenging or hostile work environment. You will need to know and adhere to the following principles, no matter what is going on at work:

- You must pray.

- You must be confident in who you are.

- You must know your mission.

- You must know why you are working and for whom you work.

- You must know how to conduct yourself in the workplace at all times.

- You must know your company's policies/procedures.

- You should know what resources are available.

- You should know the importance of mentoring.

- You must know what your Creator says about you.

You Must Pray. Daily Prayer/Devotion

Chapter 7 will discuss, in greater detail, the importance of prayer and how to develop an effectual, fervent prayer life (James 5:16). This current section speaks about a shorter time in prayer as part of devotion and making this a regular part of your preparation for work. This devotion time will set the tone for your day and your life. This time does not have to be an hour long, although you will find that the more you pray, the more time you will devote to this each day. The more you practice being in the presence of God, the more you will want to be in His presence. But initially, start out with just a few minutes where you read a scripture or other prepared reading that's scripturally based, such as a devotional, sing a bit of a praise/worship song, and then pray. As part of the prayer time, spend one to five minutes being silent, waiting for the Lord to speak. Be flexible and open to the move of the Holy Spirit. He may rearrange the order in which you proceed.

You Must Be Confident in Who You Are

We have already discussed who you are in Christ—new and perfect (whole and complete). This knowledge of who you are in Christ will empower you to be yourself and not be forced into a category by office politics and cliques.

Along with knowing who I am in Christ, knowing my personal and familial history has also brought me great comfort and has, without fail, calmed me in some chaotic situations.

In 2009, I was blessed to have my maternal family's history published in a work entitled *From Whence They Came: the Genealogical History of an African American Family*.[6] In this book, I document the struggles and triumphs of eight generations of my family, beginning with my great-great-great-grandmother Eular, a slave woman on a plantation in Virginia.

Whenever I find myself shaken by the vicissitudes of life, I remind myself of the Jesus in me and, sometimes, of the Barton, Burdette, Gibson, and Dansby in me. There have been times when I found myself thinking I just couldn't make it because of the unfairness of life. During these times, I remind myself of what my great-great-great-grandmother Eular and other family members had to endure. Then I know I can withstand whatever the enemy throws my way.

This knowledge is empowering! I cannot overstress the importance of knowing your family history, no matter how good or bad it might be.

Another aspect of knowing who you are is knowing where to draw your line in the sand at work. You must determine early on what you are and are *not* willing to do to be successful or get along. The earlier you make this decision, the easier it will be when you are confronted with challenging decisions. If you demonstrate uncertainty when it comes to ethical or legal issues, you convey that you *might,* just *might,* be willing to do something unethical or illegal to get ahead, and this challenge will keep coming up.

Early in my law enforcement career, I made it clear I was not going to "sleep" my way to success. I was not going to idly sit by and listen to racist or sexist jokes. I was not going to maliciously sabotage others' careers or stab them in the back, and I was not going to be aware of wrongdoing by other cops and not say anything. In both major law enforcement agencies in which I was employed, this made me, at times, very unpopular and, I have been told, extremely intimidating.

I was once told by a higher-ranking officer that I did not have the "right relationship" because I "wouldn't play," and because of this, I was only going to go so far in the organization. The fact that I was more educated and had more experience than many who outranked me was only moderately, if at all, considered when assignments and promotions occurred.

I have to admit: there have been times I was immensely disappointed that I did not get the latest promotion or the coveted assignment. But when I considered the possible reasons as to why it did not occur, I was settled within myself as to where I had drawn my line.

One word of caution: even though you set a standard for yourself and draw your line as to what you will and will not do, you also must be determined not to criticize others who are willing to do what you are not willing to do to move up the ladder. Everyone you work with and for has different agendas and different motivations. Each one of them has drawn their line in the sand, whether they consciously realize it or not, and it is their right to do so. You, on the other hand, have no right to determine what is or is not appropriate for someone else.

As it relates to my former law enforcement career, I made the decision that I was willing to come in an hour or two early or work an hour or two late when circumstances dictated. However, I was not willing to come in early or work late as a rule of thumb. There were just too many other areas of my life that needed my attention, and every moment was valuable to me. I did not subscribe to the old military adage that "if you're on time, you're late." I felt and still feel that "to be on time" means just that: be in the appointed place a few minutes before the appointed time.

I found myself overly critical of one person in particular who came to work hours early every day and stayed hours later than necessary. I admit I would think of terms like "kissing up" and "he needs to get a life." The point is, this was the standard he had set for himself, and I had no right to criticize what he was doing.

Success is self-defined, and each person's journey to success will be different. I had no idea how this person defined success, so I had no idea what it would take for him to attain his success. A few years later, when this person and I were competing for promotion, he got it, despite my having about ten years more experience and considerably more education. I am confident that his willingness to work longer hours played a part in his getting promoted instead of me.

Matthew 7:1 (NKJV) tells us to "judge not, that you be not judged." The Greek word used here for "judge" is *krino*. It speaks to a critical spirit, and as a Christian, my spirit should not be one of criticizing or condemning others. It should instead be an eagerness to edify and restore. The next few verses remind us that no one is so accomplished or so sound in our standing or so without fault that we can afford to criticize others. This scripture reminded me that rather than looking at what my coworker was doing and criticizing him, I should have been looking at myself and examining my own motives for what I was or was not doing. I'm glad to say that the self-assessment revealed that I had the right definition of success for *me* and that my plan of action was in alignment with the will of God. But I had not wholly committed myself to success God's way. That's why I was critical. The self-examination also revealed that I was indeed afraid that my coworker would achieve his success before I achieved mine. I was critical because what he was doing was working for him, and I was envious and resentful of him.

Once I made this admission to myself, I repented and asked for forgiveness from the Lord. I then recommitted myself to my definition of success and doing it God's way. This released a burden from me that I did not even know I was trying to carry, and it reminded me of who I was in Christ. Yes, knowing who you are will steady you, will calm you, will vitalize you, and will center you.

You Should Know Your Mission

If you are working only for money, position, or title, you will be disappointed—a lot! That is why it is crucial to know what your mission is. When I received this revelation, it started me on a journey of self-discovery. As I considered what my mission was, from a very broad perspective, I determined, according to Acts 1:8, that my mission is to witness for Him, not just to get paid. Additionally, I considered that according to Matthew 25:21–23, my mission is to be faithful to whatever the Lord puts into my hands, no matter how small or insignificant it may appear.

And finally, according to Psalm 37:23–24, my mission is advanced when I know that my steps are ordered.

This got me started in the right direction, but I was still uncertain as to how to live these principles out daily in my life. In order for me to walk in my mission, I needed more structure and a more detailed guideline.

In 2002, I attended a seminar based on Stephen Covey's *The 7 Habits of Highly Effective People*. During that training, I learned Covey's definition of a mission statement and how to create one. As I took my first attempts at creating a mission statement, I realized that I, just like most of us, have various roles I am obliged to fill. To create a genuine, self-revealing document, I would have to address all the areas of my life. Each role was important and needed its own place in my mission statement.

A mission statement focuses on what you want to be (character) and do (contributions and achievements) and on the values or principles upon which being and doing are based.[7] Writing a mission statement requires deep, honest reflection about who you are and what your purpose is. Because people are unique, each mission statement will be unique. Covey suggests that you consider the following checklist to assist you in creating a mission statement that will serve as your "constitution" for life.

Does my mission statement…

✓ define who I am?

✓ clearly establish the priority of my various roles?

✓ bring out the best in me?

✓ propel me to excellence/perfection in Christ?

I discovered I had five major roles that needed to be defined in my mission statement. They were:

• a Christian

• a wife

• a mother and grandmother

• a law enforcement officer and supervisor

• a woman

I attempt to fulfill my mission by pursuing excellence. As it relates to your work environment, this attitude of excellence will speak volumes about your professionalism and your commitment to the organization. And it will confuse your enemies!

The Benefits of Pursuing Excellence

Once I began to really strive toward excellence according to God's way, I identified several benefits in doing so.

First, *pursuing excellence demonstrates your commitment to living the best you can for the Lord.* Not always doing my best severely hinders my witness as a follower of Christ.

Another benefit of *pursuing excellence is that doing so fosters unrealized gifts that may be lying dormant within you.* You will find yourself looking for ways to do things differently and better. This will cause you to seek God for guidance, and the Holy Spirit will illuminate and stretch your thinking. Ideas will emerge. You will try new, different approaches to addressing old problems. You will realize you can multitask, you can organize better, and you can problem-solve. Your judgment and decision-making skills will either emerge or be enhanced.

When others see you operating at the top of your game in a challenging environment, it will confirm who you say you are in Christ, and they will be encouraged. Numerous times I was asked, especially by younger officers, "How do you do it? How do you keep your head up?" These kinds of questions provide an opportunity to witness about the goodness of the Lord! If they don't know Christ, it will be your chance to tell them about Him and, maybe, lead them to Him. If they already have a personal relationship with the Lord, they will be encouraged by your example.

Pursuing excellence prepares you for the next elevation. The presence of the Lord in your life should be evident in the work you do, your best work. Your employer or immediate supervisor is watching you during this time and making a note of how you respond in challenging circumstances. Pursuing excellence will demonstrate that you are poised and ready to go to the next level of responsibility.

You have demonstrated this by doing your best where you are, especially in less-than-favorable conditions. *Never minimize the place where you are. Recognize that every level is a level of preparation and maximize the experience!*

Matthew 25:21 (NKJV) says, "His lord said to him, 'Well done, good and faithful servant; you were faithful over a few things, I will make you ruler over many things. Enter into the joy of your lord.'" This well-known parable of the harsh master and the three servants with the varying amounts of talents illustrates a noticeably clear principle. *God will not elevate you to a higher position if you are not faithful in your current position.* If you are just biding your time, half-heartedly doing your job, doing just enough to get by, you are not ready for the next level of promotion/elevation. You need to demonstrate that you can produce during the best of times *and* during the worst of times. You need to demonstrate that you are not adversely affected by external circumstances. Since you are a Christian, the joy of the Lord will be your strength to do your best at all times (Nehemiah 8:10).

Pursuing excellence will cause you to draw nearer to God. Let's face it: an unfavorable, challenging, or hostile work environment will put you on your knees. Your prayer and praise life will reach new heights as you endeavor to witness for Him. You will have to seek God daily, maybe several times a day, just to keep from slapping your supervisor or coworker into next week. Believe me, there will be days you will feel like doing just that, but that would not demonstrate the love of Christ. Instead, because you have been before the Lord in prayer and praise, the Holy Spirit will quietly speak to you and keep you from doing possibly irreparable damage to your career and, most importantly, your witness. Instead of acting out of your flesh (feelings, emotions, pride), by your response, you will demonstrate that He who is in you is greater than he who is in the world (1 John 4:4). And this will confuse the enemy!

So, if you must stop in the middle of a conversation or confrontation and retreat to your office or the bathroom to keep from saying or doing something carnal (like telling them off or worse), then do so. Go in and pray!

Finally, the most important benefit of pursuing excellence is this: *it will give God glory.* And everything we do should give God glory! You set your standard for excellence and then hold yourself accountable for that standard. Never excuse yourself. *This is thriving!*

You Must Know Why You Are Working

Your employment is meant to provide a source of revenue for you to tithe, support your family, pay for education, be a blessing to others, etc. Your job may also provide a service to the community. These are all wonderful benefits.

However, if you are a Christian, you are *called* to work where you work. Whether it is a temporary position or your dream job, while you are there, you are called to exemplify the love of Christ. You do so by doing the best job you can, no matter what. You do so by being prayed up and prepared to witness about His saving grace when the opportunity presents itself.

Matthew 5:14–16 (NKJV) says,

> You are the light of the world. A city that is set on a hill cannot be hidden. Nor do they light a lamp and put it under a basket, but on a lampstand, and it gives light to all who are in the house. Let your light so shine before men, that they may see your good works and glorify your Father in heaven.

That is why it is critical to know *who you are and why you are working*. People on your job will be watching your walk, and when they find themselves in difficult situations, they will come to you for guidance. You must be ready to respond appropriately. This is your calling. This is why you are there.

In the meantime, do not expect to be appreciated by your employers or validated by your work. Expect to be paid! If you are appreciated and validated, that's a perk, a bonus, a blessing from the Lord.

You Must Know for Whom You Work

In January 2014, I retired from my job as a law enforcement officer after more than thirty-three years in the field. It was, for the most part and the vast majority of the time, an exceedingly rewarding and gratifying career. However, there were times when my work environment caused me to be physically ill (headaches, stomach problems, high blood pressure, loss of hair, weight gain). This took a devastating toll on my physical, emotional, and spiritual well-being, as well as my marriage. As I said at the beginning of this chapter, it began around 2001, and when I realized it, I immediately took action by praying and asking God for guidance.

The Lord began to speak to me through books, my pastor's sermons and Bible studies, other men and women of God, the Holy Spirit, and His Word. One of the first revelations was that I had to know for whom I worked.

As Christians, we work for the Lord. We do our work as unto the Lord (Colossians 3:23). So, no matter what is happening in the workplace, remind yourself that you represent Jesus, and everything you say and do should bring Him glory. People are watching your walk, especially during difficult times, and how you respond to challenging circumstances will speak to who you are in Him. This may be the only example of Jesus that some people will see.

The challenges continued, but I was no longer viewing them from the perspective of a victim. Instead, I knew I was victorious through Christ, and I thrived in the midst of some chaotic times. However, during an especially trying time for me, from about 2010 to 2013, it was painfully obvious to me that my supervisors, my chain of command, and my boss had failed me. I had placed my professional hopes and expectations of fulfillment in them. I had wrongfully made them responsible for providing me with something they were not able or obligated to do: to validate me and make me happy and gratified at work. I had to constantly remind myself who I was, why I was working, and for whom I worked. I typed out the following declaration and taped it right next to my computer in my office:

"I am challenged daily to respond to circumstances like Jesus" in His strength, His power, and His love. It is a process, a lifestyle, a walk, a series of moment-by-moment choices. *God is making me a visible manifestation of His power in the presence of people, and all the power that God has is presently at work inside of me.*[8] It requires *discipline, obedience, humility, and praise.* I am the righteousness of Christ (1 Corinthians 1:30). I am the aroma of Christ (1 Corinthians 4:14–21). I am more than a conqueror (Romans 8:37)."

This declaration states who Jesus is and who I am in Him; it speaks to my present and my future. Several times a day, I would read this silently or aloud or pray it. Because it was on my desk, there were times when someone would see it and ask me why it was there, what it meant, if it really helped me to have it there, etc. It was a wonderful ministry tool!

I have come to know and understand that when I find myself in treacherous circumstances, He will deliver me from the hand of the enemy, and in the meantime, He is strengthening me and preparing me for greater. He will keep me where I am until I do all I am supposed to do and/or until I learn all that I am supposed to learn from the situation. In the interim, I must endure hardships as a good soldier of Jesus Christ (2 Timothy 2:3).

You Must Know How to Conduct Yourself at All Times in the Workplace

In order to thrive in all areas of your life, what you *don't* do is just as important as what you do. So, before addressing how to act, I want to first talk about *how not to act.*

When in challenging circumstances, it is easy to adopt the persona and mindset of a victim or try too hard to get along in order to relieve pressure. But this can result in a less-than-desirable outcome. You will appear weak and vulnerable and become a target for further attack. To prevent this devastating consequence and always exude a professional demeanor, *do not act like a victim.*

Second Corinthians 2:14–16 (NKJV) says,

> Now thanks be to God who always leads us in triumph in Christ, and through us diffuses the fragrance of His knowledge in every place. For we are to God the fragrance of Christ among those who are being saved and among those who are perishing. To the one we are the aroma of death leading to death, and to the other the aroma of life leading to life. And who is sufficient for these things?

This scripture clearly states that in Christ, *we always win.* You are a warrior, victorious. Acting like a victim is contrary to the Word of God. Playing the part of the victim conveys that you are at the mercy of your environment. As a woman or man of God, you should impact the environment and not allow a negative environment to impact you. When you show up, things should change for the better. As a Christian, your life should be a living version of the gospel of Christ. Your actions should be that of a conqueror (Romans 8:37). Your actions should demonstrate that you trust God and that you know all things are working together for your good (Romans 8:28). Your actions should display that nothing that is said or done to you will cause you to fear because you know God is in control (Isaiah 54:17). Your actions should display your trust in your Jehovah. So, be strong in the Lord and in the power of His might (Ephesians 6:10).

Do not "shuck and jive."

Unless you are a comedienne, your job is not to entertain the folks at work with your wit and talent. This is not to say you should never engage in clean, pleasant, funny conversations or occasionally tell a funny story (always done in good taste and never victimizing anyone, of course). But you should not be the jokester, always trying to make people laugh. People will abuse this and go from laughing *with you* to laughing *at you*.

If you are a woman working in a male-dominated profession such as law enforcement, the military, construction, corporate, or legal fields, continuous, frivolous joking perpetuates the idea held by many of your male counterparts that you are there for their entertainment and that you should not be taken seriously. It makes it easier for your peers to ignore you and easier for your superiors to abuse you, whether consciously or unconsciously.

There is something inherently undignified and unprofessional about always joking and "clowning around" in the workplace. This type of behavior strips you of your legitimacy. Your subordinates, peers, and superiors will not take you seriously when you need them to.

Also, you should never attempt to solidify your position with members of one culture by demeaning or attempting to discredit another culture by making them the brunt of racist or sexist jokes. This type of behavior indicates a weakness in your character, and it may indicate you are willing to do other unscrupulous things as well. Others may laugh *with* you at the time, but this type of behavior sets you up as the next target. When that occurs, you will not be taken seriously when you complain because you have been guilty of doing the same to others.

So, if you want to entertain your coworkers and dazzle them with your brilliant talent, wait for the office talent show, and even then, God should get the glory!

Do not gossip.

When in a challenging environment, you may be tempted to talk to others in order to find out what, if anything, they know about your situation. This can backfire and lead you down a path of criticizing your bosses and others you feel responsible for your situation.

Beware! People who gossip *with* you will gossip *about* you and may even exaggerate or lie about you to gain favor with the boss. Don't give them anything to work with. A harmless statement you make will have gone through many revisions and additions as it moves from one person to another, and the final version may bear little resemblance to what you originally said. However, you will still be identified as the author. Never gossip, even in the best of times! It leads to a bad reputation, and it does not glorify God!

Do not sabotage.

Anger and fear may cause you to want to get even with those who you believe are responsible for your predicament. Don't do it! Leave them in the hands of the Lord.

Psalm 37:7–9 (NKJV) says,

> Be still before the Lord and wait patiently for him; do not fret when men succeed in their ways, when they carry out their wicked schemes. Refrain from anger and turn from wrath; do not fret—it leads only to evil. For evil men will be cut off, but those who hope in the Lord will inherit the land.

There is a promise attached to waiting on the Lord. Psalm 40:1 (NKJV) says, "I waited patiently for the Lord; *he turned to me and heard my cry.*"

As a Christian, you are to pursue excellence at all times, even in the worst of times. Sabotage is cruel, ruthless, underhanded, wicked, and beneath a child of the Most High God! When all is said and done, you should be able to look back over the entirety of the circumstances and see how the Lord moved on your behalf. He does not need your help. He is well able to perfect all things concerning you. Don't try to get even!

How to Act

Now that we have discussed how not to act, let us move on to how to act. The following principles apply at all times in the workplace but are especially beneficial to your witness for the Lord in a challenging work environment.

Be professional!

Do your job. Always strive for optimum performance. Never do just enough to get by. Be willing to do more than what your job description says. Strive for excellence. Remember: you work for the Lord, and you should always give Him your best!

Be wise in your speaking!

Colossians 4:5–6 (NKJV) admonishes us to "walk in wisdom toward those who are outside, redeeming the time. Let your speech always be with grace, seasoned with salt, that you may know how you ought to answer each one." I believe the reference to salt means your conversations should be amiable, relevant, life-affirming, and/or piercing the conscience, causing others to be drawn to Christ. Being wise in your speaking could mean not saying anything at all. Seek the Holy Spirit for guidance on a regular basis, and you will know when to speak and when to be silent! You don't have to respond verbally to every accusation or attack.

Be approachable and courteous!

When working in a challenging environment, it would be easy to be suspicious of everyone, develop a bad attitude, and treat everybody with disdain. This would be the human, natural response but the spiritual, godly response to a challenging environment is to demonstrate the love of Christ. One method of doing so is to be courteous and approachable to all those with whom you work, even if they are responsible for your challenging work environment.

Proverbs 15:1 (NKJV) says, "A soft answer turns away wrath, but a harsh word stirs up anger." As God's representative, you don't want to be the one stirring up anger. My great-grandmother Elizabeth Burdette would say, "Kill 'em with kindness." Okay, you don't really want to kill them, but you want to demonstrate the love of Christ, even to your enemies. I will admit: this is hard to do! It will require prayer for your enemies. Yes, that's what I said: pray for those you know who have lied about you, mistreated you, plotted your demise, planned your downfall, and schemed to prevent you from progressing in your career.

Prayer changes circumstances, and most importantly, it will change you, your mindset, and your heart. There is no way you can pray for someone and continue to be angry with them, no matter how badly they have wronged you. I know of which I speak.

During a time in my career as a law enforcement officer, I was particularly challenged by a supervisor whom I knew had prevented me from getting some desired assignments and had hindered my promotion. I remember very clearly the day the Lord told me to pray for him. I literally said out loud to the Holy Spirit, "I'm not praying for him. I *am not* that holy." When I recall my obnoxious, disobedient attitude, I am so grateful for the mercy and long-suffering of God!

Within a few days, I submitted my prideful attitude to the will of God and began to pray for the person. At first, my prayers went something like this, "Okay, Lord, I'm praying for [I'll call him 'Bob'] because You said to, but I don't want to. Anyway, he's Your creation, do something with him."

Gradually, my heart changed, and I began to pray for Bob's salvation, for the Lord to keep him and even bless him, and for the Lord to show me how to be a blessing to him. Within about three months, I learned Bob was extremely ill with a life-threatening disease, and then I began to pray for his healing.

I eventually got promoted, and Bob was now my peer; he and I worked on several projects together, all of which were highly successful. I continued to pray for him, but now I did it because I wanted to and not because it was the right thing to do. One day, he called me and told me he was making arrangements for his funeral service and asked if I would sing. I was moved by his request and agreed to sing. About two years later, when he died, his son called to confirm that I would sing. He told me his father admired me and had spoken very highly of me. I was stunned by his words!

When all was said and done, I believe God was glorified by the relationship this colleague, and I eventually developed; I was definitely changed by my prayers for him. Praying for him helped me release the battle completely to the Lord.

I encourage you to pray for your enemies. It is empowering and will change your heart. At first, you may not be able to pray specifically for the person, but the Holy Spirit will recognize the intent of your heart and will direct you on how to effectively pray for those who have intended to harm you. Praying for those who challenge you, lie about you, and plot against you will free you up mentally, emotionally, and spiritually. Praying for them will keep the bitterness from entering your being (heart and mind). If this has already happened, praying for your enemies will remove it. You cannot pray for someone and remain the same.

You must know your company's policy/procedures.

I don't care how holy, sanctified, and anointed you are—you must know the rules by which your company operates and is governed. It is imperative you know the Word of God to excel in a challenging environment, but it is equally important that you know your company's policies and procedures and that you follow them. To be disciplined or corrected because you failed to follow the rules may not be an attack. On the other hand, if the enemy was looking for a way to come against you, you have just given him a weapon when you don't follow the rules. *Do not take shortcuts.* I don't care who else does; you don't do it. Know the rules and policies and follow them. That way, even if they want to get rid of you, they can't unless they violate their own rules to do so.

> You should know what resources
> are available: education, training,
> and networking.

Education and training increase knowledge and build your resume. They allow you to focus on positive endeavors and not be constantly thinking about challenges. Avail yourself of as much education as you can afford and as much training as the company will allow. Again, this is pursuing excellence by making yourself as knowledgeable as possible. So, get all you can!

Another valuable tool for learning is networking. Look for knowledgeable people and opportunities to interact with and learn from their experience. Look for people who excel in their work and their attitudes despite the challenges they have encountered. Be selective with whom you connect. It will profit you nothing to associate yourself with persons who are bitter, disgruntled, and those who do just enough to get by. Mediocrity breeds failure and discontent!

For encouragement, look for and connect with other Christians. I cannot overstate the importance of fellowship with people of faith when in a challenging work environment. Having someone to encourage you or to keep you from doing something you might later regret is a priceless resource. It's true that one can chase a thousand and that two can put ten thousand to flight (Deuteronomy 32:30)!

From 2010 to 2011, one of my coworkers began to come to me because she felt she was being discriminated against and persecuted by her supervisor. On the first two or three occasions when she came to my office, she was either on the verge of tears or was so angry she was contemplating quitting her job. We would talk, and she would pull herself together. I encouraged her to make sure she was doing her job to the best of her ability and that she was following the office's policies. (By the way, she was. She was a consummate professional.) In as much that I was the person responsible for writing, revising, and interpreting policy, I was able to give her reliable guidance and feedback when she had questions concerning policy.

It must be noted that her supervisor never accused her of violating policy or not doing her job. Her accusations consisted of my coworker not being loyal to her supervisor, not liking her supervisor, not socializing with her, and other such nonsense. My coworker's job performance was never criticized, and there was never any disciplinary or corrective action taken against her, only a constant criticizing of her personally.

Each time when we talked, I would try to give her an appropriate scripture for the situation, and we would end our conversation with prayer. This went on for about a year, and then, in 2011, my coworker and I decided to meet every Monday morning before work to have a short devotion and prayer. We took turns selecting a scripture, expounding on it, and then praying before going to work. We spent about twenty minutes talking about the things of God (His faithfulness, His love for us, His protection over us, etc.). We said nothing about our supervisors or the negative environment. We did, however, pray for our supervisors and the challenging conditions. It set the tone for the week.

The problems continued for my coworker, but she was not adversely affected by it as she had initially been. She dealt with her supervisor in a calm, professional manner, and it infuriated the supervisor. There were times the supervisor could be heard yelling at my coworker, often on the verge of hysteria, but my coworker handled it with supreme dignity.

We continued our weekly prayer for about a year. In 2012, I was abruptly transferred from that position to a much less desirable one. I am convinced that the year we spent praying together enabled me to make the transition with peace. That year of prayer with my coworker was a time of preparation for what would be another two years of continued challenges for me. Because we worked at different locations and on different shifts, we weren't able to continue our weekly prayer time. We did, however, continue to send one another encouraging emails and an occasional phone call, and of course, we prayed for each other.

You must know the importance of mentors.

As stated above, having someone to connect with on a regular basis is helpful in dealing with a stressful work environment but having a mentor goes one step beyond that. A mentor is someone who has had similar circumstances as well as additional experience and/or education beyond what you have. They are willing to share that information with you and even guide you through your challenges.

A mentor should be someone wiser than you, someone who shares similar values, a person of faith who has demonstrated in their personal and professional lives the principles we discuss in this book.

A mentor should be someone you trust, someone who will be candid with you at all times. A true mentor will tell you when you are wrong and will not commiserate with you. She will not encourage you to feel sorry for yourself but will instead encourage you to take positive, constructive action.

A true mentor will not allow you to dwell on the challenging, negative situation but will instead encourage you to look for positive solutions. A true mentor will not engage with you in "bad-mouthing" your supervisors or the company.

A true mentor must be secure in her self-awareness. This will enable her to be transparent with you, sharing her experiences, even her mistakes, in an effort to help you. During the challenging times in my professional life, there were two persons who mentored me and were instrumental in not allowing me to sink into a pit of despair. Every time I called or met with either of them and tried to talk about how bad things were, both would direct the conversation onto a positive track, talking instead about what *I* was doing that was encouraging or elevating. Both would suggest resources for me and share how they had dealt with similar circumstances.

Proverbs 13:20 (NKJV) says, "He who walks with wise men will be wise, but the companion of fools will be destroyed." I am convinced that the counsel I received from these two very wise Christian men was instrumental in my not committing "professional" suicide.

You must commit to mentoring.

One of the many benefits of having a true mentor is that it causes you to want to be a mentor. My mentors' genuine concern and commitment to me made me aware of my obligation to help someone else and go beyond the few minutes of giving encouragement and advice and invest more deeply in the lives of those who came to me. I did this first by praying for them. I made a point to follow up with most of them on a regular basis and made myself available even during the most inconvenient times. In doing so, I discovered a wonderful benefit of mentoring others: it takes your eyes off yourself and allows you to see others' potential.

Initially, the lack of female mentors for me was quite discouraging. Those women who were in a position to mentor me based on their experience, education, level of authority, and success, chose not to. They suffered from what I called the "queen bee" syndrome. They were the queen bee in their areas, and they didn't want anyone else aspiring to their level of success. Nevertheless, their lack of encouragement motivated me, and I vowed I would not treat others, especially other women, in this manner. I looked for opportunities to encourage others.

I believe we have an obligation to help someone else keep from making the mistakes we have made. If we can make someone else's path a little easier to walk, *we should*. If we can in any way help someone else reach their fullest potential, *we should.* You won't be blessed if you are not a blessing to others. Start at once to mentor someone and expect the unexpected. Her life will change, and so will yours.

I believe mentoring (praying for, encouraging, advising, and correcting) is essential in thriving amid challenging circumstances. Mentoring is the catalyst that ignites life-affirming events. You mentor someone; they mentor someone else; that person mentors another, and so on. You mentoring one person can impact the lives of thousands!

A New Attitude

When you start to walk and talk in this new attitude of knowing (who you are, your mission, why you are working and who you work for, how to act, your company policy, what resources are available, and the importance of mentoring), the pressure will intensify! You have now become a greater threat to the enemy, and you will be attacked! How you respond is critical to your professional, personal and spiritual well-being. But relax. Don't panic! I can tell you how to not just survive in this atmosphere but how to *thrive* in it. When you respond appropriately, you will be better, and the atmosphere will change for the better. After all, you are the aroma of Christ (2 Corinthians 2:14–16).

You Must Know What Your Creator Says about You

Mistakes

At times you find yourself working in a challenging environment because of something you did wrong. Let's face it: we all make mistakes that can sometimes have devastating effects. Professionally, mistakes can result in various levels of disciplinary action and hinder your upward mobility. Personally, mistakes can result in damaged familial relationships, the loss of friends, and unplanned and unwanted life-altering consequences. Mistakes have the potential to cripple us. But I believe mistakes, no matter how bad and whether personal or professional, are not excuses for you to give up or give in to self-defeat or to live a life of mediocrity. Don't be fooled into thinking that you messed up so badly that there is no way to overcome it. It is a lie of the enemy! Instead of believing the worst, what the enemy says about you, believe the best, *what your Creator says about you.*

The Best

- You are not alone. The Lord will never leave you nor forsake you (Deuteronomy 31:6–8).

- What is ahead of you is greater than what is behind you (Job 42:12).

- There is a definite plan for your life (Jeremiah 29:11).

- If it didn't kill you, it will make you stronger and wiser after having endured it, whatever it is (Romans 5:1–5).

- All things work together for your good (Romans 8:28).

- The greatness in you will be perfected (Philippians 1:6).

What God Says about You

You will need the life-affirming Word of God in order to thrive! The following are just a few examples of what God says about you. If you don't know these, learn them. Write them down. Meditate on them or find others that speak to you!

"So do not fear, for I am with you; do not be dismayed, for I am your God. I will strengthen you and help you; I will uphold you with my righteous right hand" (Isaiah 41:10, NKJV).

"For thus says the Lord of hosts: 'He sent Me after glory, to the nations which plunder you; for he who touches you touches the apple of His eye'" (Zechariah 2:8, NKJV).

"And we know that all things work together for good to those who love God, to those who are the called according to His purpose" (Romans 8:28, NKJV).

"What then shall we say to these things? If God is for us, who can be against us?" (Romans 8:31, NKJV).

"Yet in all these things we are more than conquerors through Him who loved us" (Romans 8:37, NKJV).

"Being confident of this very thing, that He who has begun a good work in you will complete it until the day of Jesus Christ" (Philippians 1:6, NKJV).

"I can do all things through Christ who strengthens me" (Philippians 4:13, NKJV).

"But you are a chosen generation, a royal priesthood, a holy nation, His own special people, that you may proclaim the praises of Him who called you out of darkness into His marvelous light" (1 Peter 2:9, NKJV).

Are you shouting praises yet?

You get the idea. The Word of God is filled with promises of excellence, expectation, protection, provision, and covering for you. This is God's grace, His unmerited favor! And the favor of God will:

- elevate you to positions when you were not the best candidate, not the best qualified, and for which you may not be prepared. My baby brother, Minister Rodney Wilson, likes to remind me that God doesn't call the qualified; He qualifies the called.

- give you a promotion, a project, or an assignment you didn't deserve or earn.

- make up the difference/make up for your deficiencies.

- cause your enemies to bless you.

As Christians, when we make mistakes, we go to our Father, who is long-suffering, thank Him for forgiveness, and then move on. How do you move on? How do you thrive in this environment?

- Get back up. Try again.

- Never let 'em see you sweat. No matter how you feel (angry, sad, oppressed, depressed, mistreated, cheated, wronged, or a failure), act as if everything is all right! During one of the most turbulent times of my life, although not work-related, my grand-mother, Mrs. Leslie B. Cain, gave me this simplistic yet profound advice. What she was telling me was to believe God, trust God and walk in faith. One way of demonstrating that you believe Him and trust Him is by not falling apart for everybody to see. Act as if everything is all right, and it will be!

- Continue to perform at your optimum level. Always do the best job you can. Never slack. Never do just enough to get by. Remember: you work for the Lord. You do your job as unto the Lord (Colossians 3:23).

- Remember: your talents, gifts, and skills, will make a place for you (Proverbs 18:16).

- Project a positive attitude. Make them wonder how you can be so calm in the midst of chaos, disaster, and treachery (Psalm 37:7–9).

- Consider this: crisis becomes opportunity when you respond appropriately. You may have the opportunity to witness about the saving power of Jesus. It was in my most frenzied times that I had someone come to me and ask, "How do you do it? How do you keep your head up? How do you keep from going off, knowing what they did to you?" Questions like these open the door for you to witness about the saving and *keeping grace* of God.

A challenging work environment will definitely present the opportunity to demonstrate that you can perform professionally, graciously, and flawlessly under pressure. As I said before, your "bosses" are watching how you respond in challenging circumstances. It is quite probable that the next time a major project, assignment, or incident presents itself, you will be considered because of how you responded to an initial challenge. This could catapult you to promotion. Even if it doesn't, you have represented your Father in a manner that gives Him glory, and that is our purpose for being.

Assess the crisis. If it is of an ethical nature, this is your opportunity to demonstrate you *will not* commit any unethical acts, and if this type of crisis is common at your place of employment, it may be the opportunity for you to look for employment elsewhere.

Now that you know what your Creator says about you, there are some practical things you must do before going to work and some things to do while at work. These practices will allow you to walk in the knowledge of who you are in Christ.

Devotion

As discussed earlier in the section "You Must Pray," I suggest you begin with a portion of a song, a scripture reading, and a prayer of praise and thanksgiving. Another aspect of my preparation for work (I am now retired) and a regular portion of my prayer time is to verbally recite the weapons of my warfare. I typically say, "Now Lord,

I place upon myself Your full armor as outlined in Ephesians 6:10–18: the belt of truth, the breastplate of righteousness, the gospel of peace, the shield of faith, the helmet of salvation, and the sword of the Spirit, which is the Word of God. Praying with all prayer and supplication, I put on the Lord Jesus Christ [Romans 13:14], a robe of righteousness [Isaiah 61:10], the glory of God is my rear guard [Isaiah 58:8], and the joy of the Lord is my strength [Nehemiah 8:10]."

Again, all of this will only take a few minutes before you depart for work.

Praise Break

Take praise breaks throughout the day. If you have an office, close the door and spend just a few minutes, or a few seconds, just thinking about the goodness of the Lord. Begin to thank Him for His love, His protection, His mercy, His grace, His loving-kindness, etc. Make a melody in your heart unto the Lord. Sing a song! You may not be able to do it out loud, but you can do it quietly, humming to yourself that one special song that always ushers you into His presence. It creates quick access to that intimate place in your spirit you have reserved exclusively for God.

If you do not have an office, find a quiet place like the bathroom, break room, or workout area when no one else is there. I want to stress to take *just a few minutes*.

When a situation is about to escalate to the point of hostility by you or the other person involved, excuse yourself! If you know you are about to "go off" and you are about to demonstrate un-Christlike or unprofessional behavior, excuse yourself! Ask for a short break, go to the bathroom, or make any excuse to distance yourself from the source of aggravation. And then pray! Now, you can't stay in the bathroom for an hour, but three to five minutes is all it will take for you to gather yourself, to regroup. When I didn't have an office, I spent a *lot* of time in the bathroom! And when the door to my office was closed, everyone knew not to disturb me for about five minutes.

Weekly Consecration

In 2013, I began practicing a day of consecration. I set aside
one day a week where I isolate myself as much as possible from
all outside influences. For me, this means no television (unless
something spiritual such as one of the programs on Christian
television), no news, no Facebook, no text, no phone calls (unless
critical), and no frivolous reading. I feed my spirit nothing but
spiritual things. I read nothing but the Word or other spiritual, life-
giving, inspirational material; I listen only to Gospel music; I work
on sermons or Bible study lessons, and I work on other uplifting
things (like *ICIT*)!

If you are married, try to arrange this day around your husband's
schedule so it will not in any way interfere with what he may need
from you. Maintain your wifely chores such as cooking, cleaning, and
laundry but while doing so, listen to music or scriptures on audio.

Besides Sunday, my day of consecration is the most satisfying day
of the week. I look forward to it with great expectation. This day of
consecration has enhanced my life immensely!

Fasting

Let me say from the very beginning: *fasting is difficult!* But the
benefits of fasting cannot be overstated. Something happens when
you fast. For me, it is a declaration that I put my flesh (mind,
emotions, and appetites) into submission.

Fasting is extremely beneficial for the spirit (S), mind (M), and
body (B). Some of the benefits I have received from fasting are:

- A deeper intimacy between me and God the Father,
  God the Son, and God the Holy Spirit (S)

- Greater focus on the Lord and not myself (S, M)

- Greater sensitivity to the voice of the Holy Spirit (S)

- Greater revelation and understanding of the Word (S, M)

- Facilitates discipline in my prayer and study time (S, M)

- I am less likely to be easily offended. I am more conscious of how I interact with others (S, M)

- My heart is more sensitive to others (S).

- Clearer thought processes (M)

- Produces humility before God (S)

- A greater desire to seek God (S)

- Highlights my dependence on God (S)

- I am encouraged (S, M)

- Spiritual control of my flesh. My flesh will do what I say as guided by the Spirit (S, B)

There has been much debate as to whether or not a "genuine" fast is going without food or if it is acceptable to "fast" from other things such as television, Facebook, texting, etc. To answer this question, I refer you to the Word of God. Both the Hebrew (*sôm*) and Greek (*nēsteia*) words for "fast" or "fasting" mean literally "abstaining from food." I submit for your consideration that separating yourself from people, all forms of social media, entertainment, or any other activities you regularly participate in and enjoy is a time of *consecration*, as I discussed above.

If you have never fasted before, seek guidance from the Lord and read the Word daily. Also, there are hundreds, if not thousands, of resources on fasting that can be helpful. Most importantly, pray and be led by God as to what kind of fast to undertake and for how long to fast.

I am convinced that once you make fasting a regular part of your life, you will recognize one of the greatest benefits is how fasting prepares you to deal with the challenges in every area of your life. You are calmer, more in tune with the Holy Spirit, and not easily angered by the challenges to which you are subjected.

Summary

I think a summing up of this chapter is helpful to remind you that in order to thrive in a challenging work environment, you must *know* some things and *do* some other things.

First, you must know success is self-defined and each person's journey to success will be different. To define success and be successful, you need to know:

- to pray

- who you are

- your mission

- why you are working

- for whom you work

- how not to act and how to act

- your company policy/procedures

- what resources are available

- the importance of mentoring and,

- what your Creator says about you

Second, you cannot allow mistakes to cripple you for life. It is never too late to try again, and it's always too soon to give up. When you make mistakes, do the following:

- get back up,

- never let 'em see you sweat,

- continue to perform at your optimum level,

- remember: your talents, gifts, and skills will make a place for you,

- project a positive attitude,

- look for an opportunity within the crisis.

Third, know what God's Word says about you.

Finally, when you engage in the following practices, you will walk in the knowledge of who you are in Christ:

- daily devotion

- praise breaks at work

- weekly consecration

- fasting

This knowledge is empowering and will equip you to face every challenge in a manner that will bring God glory:

Action Item(s)

Merriam-Webster defines mantra as "a word or phrase that is repeated often or that expresses someone's basic beliefs."[9] This could be your favorite quote, spiritual truth, or Scripture that motivates and inspires you to be your best self.

My personal definition of "mantra" is "a self-affirming, biblically-based declaration that guides my life."

In 2007, after seeking the Holy Spirit for some time, the words "discipline," "obedience," "humility," and "praise" were continually repeated in my spirit and emerged as my mantra. Sometime in 2014, whenever I spoke my mantra, I began to hear "maximize potential." Thus, my mantra expanded to "Discipline, obedience, humility, and praise will maximize my potential!" In 2020, the year of clarity, my mantra further evolved to "Discipline, obedience, humility, and praise will maximize my potential *and create opportunity!*"

I speak my mantra often, almost daily, as it is a part of my prayer time. However, it is especially useful when I find myself troubled, confused, or unsure about anything. Speaking it out loud causes me to refocus, and it reminds me of who I am in Christ.

I encourage you to develop a mantra for your life. This may take some time because you need to pray and ask the Holy Spirit for guidance. Until you develop your mantra, you can *personalize* your favorite encouraging scripture. For example, you can change Isaiah 54:17 to say, "No weapon formed against *me* shall prosper, and every tongue which rises against *me* in judgment *I* shall condemn. This is *my* heritage as a servant of the Lord, and *my* righteousness is from Him, says the Lord."

Type out your mantra or declaration and place it in a prominent place for you to see it several times a day or make it your screensaver on your computer. At the beginning of your day, the end of your day, and anytime you need to do so, speak it to yourself!

Another action item for this week is to begin to develop your personal definition of success. It may take some time, so don't be in a hurry. This definition, along with your mantra, will be instrumental in guiding your future actions.

Note: Be aware of your employment policies and do not put personal items on your desk or work computer if it is a violation of policy. However, you can write your mantra or declaration on index cards and place them in your locker, purse, pocket, lunch bag, etc.

Prayer

Gracious God, as I daily go into my workplace, help me remember that I am working for You. Holy Spirit, remind me that how I respond to the challenging environment has the potential to encourage or discourage others. Empower me to respond in a manner that gives You glory. In Jesus's name, I pray. Amen!

Reflections

thrive

THRIVING (HOW TO MINISTER) IN A TENSION-FILLED HOME

Act like everything's all right.

Leslie B. Cain

I need to say at the very beginning of this chapter that this book cannot address the issue of an abusive environment. In more than thirty-three years of my career as a law enforcement professional, I never saw an abusive relationship get better. I know, *in theory*, that it can get better with much prayer and if both persons are committed to doing the work to make it better. It will require the insight and guidance of trained professionals, and for that, I am not equipped. So, I will simply say that if your life is in jeopardy, find a safe place to go and then seek guidance from Holy Spirit and the professionals as to how to proceed.

This chapter addresses a tension-filled home within the context of marriage and a home environment where a woman may feel humiliated, rejected, unloved, oppressed, misunderstood, and/or subjugated. If you are in a tension-filled environment experiencing any of these conditions, and you are not married to the person, it is insanity to stay!

Even when married, you might ask, "Why would I stay in an environment like that?" That is a valid question, and there is biblical support for remaining in a tension-filled environment:

1. Marriage is a sacred relationship to the heart of God. It is the first relationship between two people established and blessed by God, second only to the relationship between God and man (Genesis 2:18–25).

2. God sees marriage between a man and woman as enduring and binding. It is the model He has chosen to demonstrate His relationship to His children, and thus, He is vehement in regard to the maintenance of the home and family (Malachi 2:16).

3. The dissolution of this one-flesh relationship leaves painful scars for all involved (Malachi 2:13–15).

4. Marriage is a covenant, and Jesus gave no divine decree for breaking this holy covenant. However, He acknowledged that in a sinful world, this tragedy does occur (Matthew 19:3–9).

5. Once forgiveness is exercised, restoration of the marriage is possible, and God gets the glory!

A tension-filled home can be far more difficult to thrive in than a challenging work environment for one simple reason; you are not as emotionally invested in the people at work as you are in your family and spouse. Because of the investment of love, you are far more vulnerable to the actions, ideas, and opinions of those in your home. Deciding to stay in a home where you feel unappreciated and maybe, unloved is one of the toughest decisions you will make, and if you stay, you will need to know how to overcome the impact

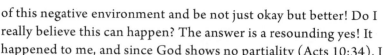

of this negative environment and be not just okay but better! Do I really believe this can happen? The answer is a resounding yes! It happened to me, and since God shows no partiality (Acts 10:34), I believe He will do the same for you.

During the time that I was writing this book, I talked to many people, mostly women, concerning what the book was about. I would briefly describe the concept of perfection and why I began the book with that explanation. Next, I would tell them about the chapter dealing with working in a challenging work environment and they would ask a couple of questions or express interest in knowing more. But when I talked about this chapter concerning living in a tension-filled home, most of the women I talked to would get a look of disbelief or excitement or fear. In several conversations, women began to cry and reveal that they were living in homes filled with tension. Many of them would go on to tell me how they had never read anything that dealt with this issue and that they were glad I was writing about it. One really good friend asked how I dared write about such a private matter.

I dared because, for years, I believed I was the only woman in my immediate circle of friends, colleagues, associates, and church family who was living in a tension-filled home. But over the course of three years and numerous conversations, I discovered I was distressingly mistaken. Many of these conversations gave me the opportunity to minister one-on-one to women who were hurting, afraid, desperate, lonely, considering divorce, considering suicide, abusing medication, abusing alcohol, and considering drastic cosmetic and/or weight loss surgery.

The demographic profiles of these women varied. They were poor and wealthy. Some had advanced degrees, and others had not graduated from high school. Some had been unwed mothers, and others had gone to college, married, had great careers, and then had their babies. Some were stay-at-home mothers, and others worked outside the home, either by choice or out of necessity. Some of them grew up in stable, nurturing two-parent households, while others were raised by single mothers or foster parents. Some had suffered emotional, physical, and sexual abuse at the hands of those who should have protected them. They were employed in various professions that included the military, education, medicine, ministry, corporate, law enforcement, judicial, criminal, and other fields.

They were Christian and nonbelievers. They ranged in age from early twenties to their seventies. They were from varied racial and ethnic backgrounds.

All of them, at one time or another, felt they were living in unbearable conditions. These women felt trapped and bound up inside, with no way out. Often, they would use terminology like, "I feel as if I'm in prison." Even now, as I recall the many women I talked to, I am flooded with emotion. I recognized and understood their pain, fear, frustration, and desperation. It is a dreadful state in which to live. It is for this reason, and after much prayer, that I decided to address the issue and share with you how I first barely survived and then thrived in this state of insanity. It was not an easy decision, and I changed my mind a few times before finding the courage to move forward with writing it down.

I looked up the word "tension" to see if the dictionary definition adequately described what I had felt during the worst moments in my marriage and what many of these women said they had felt.

The Merriam Webster's Collegiate Dictionary, Eleventh Edition, describes tension, in part, as

> the act or action of stretching or the condition or degree of being stretched to stiffness; inner striving, unrest, or imbalance often with physiological indication of emotion; a state of latent hostility or opposition between individuals or groups.[10]

The bad news here is this was a precise description of how I felt for years in my home. I had been stretched until I was stiff and cold. My inner being was in constant turmoil, strife, and unrest. One day I was fine; the next day, an emotional wreck. I constantly wavered back and forth between faith and fear, joy and sorrow, love and hate, certainty and confusion.

This state of tension was draining, and it had devastating physical, emotional, and spiritual consequences. I was sad and angry most of the time, but I put on a mask of Christian contentment. I was paranoid and fearful, wondering if my stress showed. I began to wonder if God saw what was going on and if He cared. I never doubted God! I knew He *could* change my state of being, but since He did not, I concluded I deserved what I was getting. I simply had to put my big girl panties on and tough it out.

Then one really bad day, I called my grandmother to complain to her about one specific issue with which I was struggling. I felt betrayed, humiliated, abandoned, and every other crippling emotion that you can think of. I was crying so hard that I could barely take a deep breath. At one point, I was hovering dangerously on the verge of hysteria, and then, very quietly and calmly, she said, "Act like everything's all right."

I was dumbfounded! Didn't she hear me? Didn't she understand what I was saying? I cried out, "But Mama, you don't understand. You don't know what I'm going through!" Before I could go on, she responded in that same calm voice, "You just got to trust God that He'll make everything all right. Until He does, *act like everything's all right.*"

This time when she spoke, there was a quickening, an illumination in my spirit that translated her words into, "Call those things that be not as though they were" (Romans 4:17, NKJV). She was not telling me to walk around in a state of denial but instead to walk in and live in *faith.*

I got it! I understood what she was saying. I had to trust that God saw my situation, that He understood even if I did not, and that if He was allowing it, there was something I needed to learn from it. In the meantime, I had to be thankful and worshipful. I had to remain kind in my dealings with others and especially my husband.

She continued on to tell me to pray and perform all my wifely duties with love, such as cooking, keeping my house clean, having sex regularly (she whispered this), and doing the big things and the little things. I understood and told her I was doing all these things. She asked, "Is he putting his hands on you?" I told her no. She said, "Well then, just keep doing what you're doing." She assured me the Lord would "fix it!"

Her quiet, confident assertion broke through the hysteria and calmed me. It was all so clear. Either I trusted God, or I didn't. If I did, I had to walk in assurance in that for which I believed God to do, which was to restore love, trust, passion, and cohesiveness in my home.

Sounds good, doesn't it? But now I was faced with how to actually do it.

Before outlining how I walked through the process of thriving in my tension-filled home, I want to say that it doesn't matter what the source of the tension is in your home. The same Biblical principles and common-sense approach will work and relieve the tension.

The typical sources of tension in most marriages are money and sex. It could be any aspect of these two: not enough money, not enough sex, one spouse being frugal, the other being a spendthrift, the wife making more money than the husband, infidelity, or using either money or sex to garner control in the marriage.

Some other common sources of tension in a home are career conflicts, in-laws, drug and/or alcohol abuse, severe illness, children from previous relationships/marriages, adult children, and elderly parents to care for. For the Christian having an unsaved spouse can be a tremendous source of tension.

Certainly, these are not all the sources of tension that can attack a home but again, I believe the battle plan for repelling the attack is the same. So, let us look at *how to thrive in a tension-filled home.*

Pray

I have to admit to you that prayer was not always my first thought or action. I had to learn the hard way that before saying or doing anything, I needed God's guidance. Regular, consistent prayer in your life will provide clear direction when needed, even in the most chaotic moments. Prayer should be your default position in all circumstances! I will provide more detail concerning prayer in Chapter 7.

Act like Everything Is All Right

A long time before calling Mama Leslie, I prayed about my situation, but I didn't hear from the Lord. I couldn't understand why but after our talk, I began to pray differently, and I realized that before that point, I was not *ready* to hear from God about this situation. So, instead of praying *about* my husband, I began to pray *for* my husband. I stopped outlining all my husband's faults, failures, and shortcomings and asked God to show me how to minister to him. I asked the Lord to show me what I was doing wrong and what I could do better. I must admit: initially, this portion of my prayer was a bit sarcastic and insincere because I didn't think I was doing anything wrong. I had been wronged. Nevertheless, I kept praying this way.

I continued to pray about my situation, and one of the first things the Holy Spirit showed me was I had to forgive, and I had to acknowledge that I needed forgiveness in the situation! Can I be really candid with you? I did not want to do either. This was hard! This brings me to the first step in acting as if everything is all right:

Forgiveness

When we ask God for forgiveness, it is immediate and complete; actually, it's already done. When Jesus shed His blood for us on Calvary, the new covenant of grace was ushered in. Listen to what Paul says.

> For if the blood of bulls and goats and the ashes of a heifer, sprinkling the unclean, sanctifies for the purifying of the flesh, how much more shall the blood of Christ, who through the

eternal Spirit offered himself without spot to God, cleanse your conscience from dead works to serve the living God?

Hebrews 9:13–14 (NKJV)

All we have to do is believe that we are completely forgiven of all our sins and that the blood of Jesus cleanses us from all unrighteousness. Christ accomplished all the forgiveness we will ever need when He died on the cross. Now all you have to do is thank Him and praise Him for it and move on. It is done!

Next, you need to forgive your spouse for whatever the offense is. It may not be easy, but it is essential to mounting an effective attack against the enemy. If the enemy can keep you in a state of not forgiving, nothing else you do will be effective. You may not be able to fully forgive all at once. For us humans, forgiveness is often a process. Ask God to complete and perfect your forgiveness concerning your spouse. Forgive! Keep working on it. To live in a state of not forgiving keeps you a victim and makes you vulnerable to the enemy.

Remember Who You Are

The next step in acting like everything is all right is to know who you are. We have already discussed who you are in Christ in Chapter 1—new, perfect creation (whole and complete). This knowledge of who you are in Christ will empower you to be strong in the Lord and the power of His might (Ephesians 6:10–18). Review Chapter 1 if you need to.

Remember You Have the Favor of God

As you continue the process of acting like everything is all right, remember: God loves you. He is pulling for you too. He is working on your behalf. Review the section in Chapter 2 entitled "What the Creator Says about You." A quick refresher follows:

- You are not alone. The Lord will never leave you nor forsake you (Deuteronomy 31:6–8).

- What is ahead of you is greater than what is behind you (Job 42:12).

- There is a definite plan for your life (Jeremiah 29:11).

- If it didn't kill you, it will make you stronger and wiser after having endured it, whatever "it" is (Romans 5:1–5).

- All things work together for your good (Romans 8:28).

- The greatness in you will be perfected (Philippians 1:6).

Just Remember

Remember past victories and how God worked on your behalf. Remember God's faithfulness toward you. Read Lamentations 3:22–24. Remember in whom you have placed your trust.

Remembering the love of God will equip you, empower you, and enable you to love in adverse conditions. Remember the victory He accomplished for us at the Cross. Remember His grace. Just remember!

Hope

As we move through this process of acting like everything is all right, hope is essential!

During the 2008 presidential election, I listened to many politicians and political pundits mock then-Senator Barack Obama's call to hope. They minimized the importance of hope and suggested that

Senator Obama was limited because hope, according to them, was the only thing he had to offer the American people. As I considered the many subtle and blatant insulting comments made toward him and his "message of hope," I screamed inside myself. I wanted to tell them all just how important hope is. I was astounded that they didn't know!

People need hope! Hope is what gets us up in the morning and makes us keep trying to make it. Hope is that intangible "thing" that we can't see, touch, taste, or smell, but without it, we can't live. There have been times in my life when hope was all I had, and it was all I needed to keep going.

My frustration at their trivializing the importance of hope led me to the Bible. I wanted to know what the Word of God had to say about hope. So, I did a search and found 158 passages of Scripture with the word "hope." The following are just a few that spoke to me.

- 1 Chronicles 29:15 (NJV) says, "For we are aliens and pilgrims before You, as were all our fathers; our days on earth are as a shadow, and without hope."

- Without hope, our lives are dark, empty, and void.

- Acts 2:26 (NKJV) says, "Therefore, my heart rejoiced, and my tongue was glad; moreover, my flesh also will rest in hope."

- Resting is being in a constant state of hope based on trust in the Lord.

- Romans 5:3–5 (NKJV) says,

And not only that, but we also glory in tribulations, knowing that tribulation produces perseverance; and perseverance, character; and character, hope. Now hope does not disappoint, because the love of God has been poured out in our hearts by the Holy Spirit who was given to us.

Hope does not disappoint.

- First Corinthians 13:13 (NKJV) says, "And now abide faith, hope, love, these three; but the greatest of these is love."

Hope is important. It ranks up there with faith and love.

- 1 Peter 1:3 says (NKJV), "Blessed be the God and Father of our Lord Jesus Christ, who according to His abundant mercy has begotten us again to a living hope through the resurrection of Jesus Christ from the dead."

Jesus is our *living hope*, which inspires and invigorates.

Trials, tribulations, troubles, and disappointments are limited, finite, and transitory, but hope is enduring, everlasting, and unending. Every area of trouble presents an opportunity to hope. Even in troubled times, hope is present and will shine through if our hope is properly placed, properly positioned in the Lord.

Hope is a necessity of life. I say that without hope, there can be no life, no change. Hope ignites the flame of change. First, we hope; then, we believe; then, we act! But our hope must be in God. My hope is firmly rooted in Jesus and His righteousness. I dare hope in Jesus because he has proven himself faithful. He is the *living hope*. So, keep trusting! Keep believing that the situation will get better because hope (Jesus) does not disappoint.

Seek Wise Counsel

As you continue to pray and act like everything is all right, your demeanor will change for the better. You have now begun to thrive in this challenging environment. However, there will be days when you need to talk to someone. Ecclesiastes 4:9–12 (NKJV) talks about the value of a friend:

> Two are better than one, because they have a good reward for their labor. For if they fall, one will lift up his companion. But woe to him who is alone when he falls, for he has no one to help him up. Again, if two lie down together, they will keep warm; but how can one be warm alone? Though one may be overpowered by another, two can withstand him. And a threefold cord is not quickly broken.

This portion of Scripture tells us that when you have a trusted friend to come into agreement, praying on any issue, there is a reward for that "labor." This principle is reinforced in Matthew 18:19–20 (NKJV):

> Again I say to you that if two of you agree on earth concerning anything that they ask, it will be done for them by My Father in heaven. For where two or three are gathered together in My name, I am there in the midst of them.

It is wise of you to seek wise counsel. When you are weary, wise counsel will lift you up with an encouraging word. However, I can't stress enough how important it is that you be *exceedingly selective* in whom you choose to confide. You will be revealing sensitive information, so the person must be someone who is trustworthy. The Amplified version of Proverbs 1:5 (AMPCE) says, "The wise also will hear and increase in learning, and the person of understanding will acquire skill and attain to sound counsel (so that he may be able to steer his course rightly)." Everyone is not able to help you carry your burden, but the wise counsel of mature, accomplished prayer warriors will help you get on track and stay on track.

I remind you that this is a war you're fighting for your peace of mind, your marriage, your children, and your family for generations to come. To wage war effectively and be victorious, you must have wise counsel (Proverbs 20:18; 24:16).

I was blessed to have the wise counsel of seven mighty women of God. First, my grandmother, Mrs. Leslie Cain, and my mother, Mrs. Marilyn Hyde, have always been safe havens for me to run to in times of trouble. Everything they ever told me was right and good and God-inspired. I only wish I had recognized that when I was sixteen and eighteen and twenty-three years of age.

In addition to my mother and grandmother, I was blessed to have in my life, during this time, Mother Bernice Harper. Not once did I seek her out, and she did not stop what she was doing and minister to me with a word of advice, correction, or prayer, and sometimes, all of these.

Another person I talked to was the Reverend Carrie Price, and she gave me a most effective tool to help maintain my sanity. She told me to "get it off my brain." I'll talk more about this later.

My friend, Reverend Savannah Jackson, was one person with whom I could always be brutally candid.

One day I was talking about fasting to the First Lady of my former church, Bernice Thompson. I told her I was "seeking the Lord for direction on fasting." She asked me how long I had been "seeking Him," and I said, "About three months." She looked at me and said, "You need to stop seeking and just do it." A few days later, she gave me a book on fasting, and it was a tremendous resource. Fasting has become a regular part of my life.

When I confided in my friend, Laura Brooks, she simply said, "I'm here for whatever you need." These few words from her reminded me I was not alone in this battle.

I am grateful to have these wise, steady, godly warrior-women in my life.

Journal (Get It off Your Brain)!

During an especially difficult period, I confided to Reverend Carrie Price about some of my frustrations. She asked me if I wrote in a journal, and I told her no. I did a lot of writing for sermon and Bible lesson preparation and on various ideas I had for future literary work, but I never seriously utilized writing as a therapeutic tool. When I told her this, she said, "Write it all down; get it off your brain!"

I went home that evening and wrote down the last specific incident that had been troubling me and was immediately relieved! I was amazed that writing it down really validated and diminished the pain. No matter how hurtful the issue had been in the saying or doing of it, once I wrote it down in my journal, the pain was relieved.

Writing it down allowed me to release it from my inner being. I could say whatever I wanted to say and not have to defend it or listen to a rebuttal. Writing it down either legitimized my pain or helped me realize when I was seeing things from a one-sided perspective. I was able to better identify and admit when I was being unfair and easily offended as opposed to having been legitimately injured.

Writing it down caused me to look at the issue more objectively and be honest with myself about the true severity of the offense. Writing helped me realize when I was wrong and made it easier for me to admit it, first in the writing and then to my husband.

Writing allowed me to focus on whatever the issue was for a few minutes or maybe even a few hours, but once it was written down, it was out of me and no longer an object of my attention. Writing it down got it off my brain; I was not constantly thinking about it. Essentially, once I wrote about an issue, I seldom thought about it again. If I did, I would go back, read the entry again and dismiss it. I was surprised how at one time, a particular thing said or done had been so debilitating for me but later had little, if any, harmful effect. A lot of what I had written I had completely forgotten about and had forgiven the injury.

Another benefit of writing down your thoughts is a recall of the good. Don't just write down the negative things. Write down what you believe God to do in your life. Record what your dreams and aspirations are. This is helpful on really bad days when you can't remember what you prayed for. If you can't call it to mind because things have gotten so bad, you can read it again and remind yourself. Read it out loud. Make a declaration to yourself and to the enemy.

Writing it down brought clarity, truth, and immediate inward peace!

Your journaling can be written to yourself, which becomes a means of encouraging yourself, or you can write to God, which becomes prayer. Both methods are effective. Just get it off your brain!

Communication. Talk to Your Spouse

For a long time, I was reluctant to talk to my husband about serious matters because we usually ended up arguing. I was frustrated because I needed him to *understand* my viewpoint and not just listen to what I was saying; I needed him to acknowledge when I was right. When this didn't happen, we would go back and forth, both vying for control. This most often ended with harsh words and hurt feelings for both of us.

It wasn't until I began to pray right and walk in knowing who I was in the Lord, that I came to realize two things. First, I didn't always have to have my say. It was okay for me not to say anything, to shut up! I know this was from the Holy Spirit because I would have never reached this conclusion on my own. *I always felt I had to be heard.*

The second thing I realized was my husband did not have to agree with me or acknowledge that my concerns were legitimate. When I felt I *really* had to say something, I learned to say it in a nonconfrontational tone and walk away. I did not have to be validated by him. This took a while, but when I got it, it liberated me. It reminded me of something the elders used to say when I was a child: "Giving up your right for the wrong."

Sometimes neither of you is wrong. You just have different perspectives, and thus, you will not agree. So, you have to agree to disagree without deliberately trying to hurt one another or play the part of a victim.

At times walking away is good, but eventually, you must talk to each other. Disagreements do not have to turn into arguments. Open, honest communication will keep this from happening. Agree on rules of engagement before addressing serious topics or topics you know have the potential to get heated. Some basic rules are:

- no yelling

- no cursing

- no name calling

- no purposely hurtful things said

- Don't go over the same things over and over again. (I was guilty of this.) First Corinthians 13:5 reminds us that love keeps no record of wrong.

- Agree to walk away if things get heated and come back later. Ephesians 4:26–27 (NKJV) states, "Be angry, and do not sin: do not let the sun go down on your wrath, nor give place to the devil." It is okay to walk away for a while but don't let anger linger. It leaves a wide-open door for the enemy to attack your emotions.

- When you are wrong, say, "I was wrong and am sorry."

All this sounds really good and does actually work *if* both parties agree. But what if your spouse does not agree to these rules? In that case, you make every attempt to talk without nagging and suggest other healing activities. But if he does not agree, you keep doing what you know is right and beneficial to do: pray, fast, maintain your home, and seek counseling together from your pastor or Christian marriage counselor. Know that you have done all you can do to be a ministering agent and facilitate peace in your home (Romans 12:18).

However, if your spouse will not agree to counseling, you go and, as much as you are able, do what they suggest (exercises, writing, etc.). Be brutally honest. Be candid. This is not the time to act like everything is all right. A professional counselor will give you objective feedback, but they must have all the pertinent information from which to advise you. Talking to a professional is another way to get it off your brain and to release past buried offenses.

During this time, I read 1 Corinthians 13 over and over and over again. This might be a good time for you to do that:

The Greatest Gift

Though I speak with the tongues of men and of angels, but have not love, I have become sounding brass or a clanging cymbal. And though I have the gift of prophecy, and understand all mysteries and all knowledge, and though I have all faith, so that I could remove mountains, but have not love, I am nothing. And though I bestow all my goods to feed the poor, and though I give my body to be burned, but have not love, it profits me nothing. Love suffers long and is kind; love does not envy; love does not parade itself, is not puffed up; does not behave rudely, does not seek its own, is not provoked, thinks no evil; does not rejoice in iniquity, but rejoices in the truth; bears all things, believes all things, hopes all things, endures all things. Love never fails. But whether there are prophecies, they will fail; whether there are tongues, they will cease; whether there is knowledge, it will vanish away. For we know in part and we prophesy in part. But when that which is perfect has come, then that which is in part will be done away. When I was a child, I spoke as a child, I understood as a child, I thought as a

In Christ I Thrive

child; but when I became a man, I put away childish things. For now we see in a mirror, dimly, but then face to face. Now I know in part, but then I shall know just as I also am known. And now abide faith, hope, love, these three; but the greatest of these is love.

1 Corinthians 13:1–13 (NKJV)

It may be very beneficial for you to read the NIV and Amplified versions of this scripture as well. I read them all!

Consider it a privilege to be the one to walk in love. No, I'm not crazy, and yes, I really do mean it when I say it is a privilege to be the one fighting the battle.

Let God Be God in Your Spouse's Life

If your spouse is saved but doesn't attend church as regularly as you do, do not be critical of him, not even in your mind. Do not look down on him when he doesn't want to go to church.

The enemy will use this to build up resentment in you and give you the idea that you're smarter, stronger, a better Christian, and "more saved." Don't give the enemy this inch. It could turn into a gaping gulf in your home. Be at peace with him being his own man. Be at peace with his manner of service. Let God be God in his life!

If your spouse is not saved, you have the opportunity to win him to Christ by your witness. In 1 Corinthians 7:10–16 (NKJV), Paul admonishes us,

Now to the married I command, yet not I but the Lord: A wife is not to depart from her husband. But even if she does depart, let her remain unmarried or be reconciled to her husband. And a husband is not to divorce his wife. But to the rest I, not the Lord, say: If any brother has a wife who does not believe, and she is willing to live with him, let him not divorce her. And a woman who has a husband who does not believe, if he is willing to live with her, let her not divorce him. For the unbelieving husband is sanctified by the wife, and the unbelieving wife is sanctified by the husband; otherwise your children would be unclean, but now they are holy. But if the unbeliever departs, let him depart; a brother or a sister is not under bondage in such cases. But God has called us to peace. For how do you know, O wife, whether you will save your husband? Or how do you know, O husband, whether you will save your wife?

Here in this passage of Scripture, Paul is telling us that the presence of one saved spouse in the home makes it a Christian home and marriage, and everything should be done to keep the home intact. It could be that the unsaved spouse will come to the Lord because of their relationship with the saved spouse.

Peter echoes a similar sentiment in 1 Peter 3:1–4 (NKJV). It reads,

Wives, likewise, be submissive to your own husbands, that even if some do not obey the word, they, without a word, may be won by the conduct of their wives, when they observe your chaste conduct accompanied by fear. Do not let your adornment be merely outward—arranging the hair, wearing gold, or putting on fine apparel—rather let it be the hidden person of the heart, with the incorruptible beauty of a gentle and quiet spirit, which is very precious in the sight of God.

Peter is telling us here that the unsaved husband may be won by observing the Christian lifestyle of his wife. In verse 2, the word "fear" speaks to reverence for God and respect for your husband. Peter goes on to tell us not to put our faith in our outward beauty. He is not condemning taking care of yourself and how you look to your husband. He is, however, telling us that we are not to be dependent on those attributes but to trust in Christ and the cross.

Intimacy

Once, I was out of my two favorite perfumes, and without telling me, my husband bought them both and put them on the dresser. It took me several days to notice. I was ashamed, and he was hurt. For him, this was a prelude to intimacy and very important…and I missed it. It was an opportunity for me to minister to my husband in a way that only I can, and I missed it! I realized how important it was for me to acknowledge and respond appropriately to the big and the small things he does, especially since he was making an effort to please me.

This brings me to the following point: Husbands, you have the tremendous power to shift the atmosphere in your home with one word or one act. You have the God-given power to impact the destiny of your wife, your children, and your entire family for generations. It is a tremendous responsibility, and it takes a God-led man to accomplish this.

One sure way to decrease the tension in a home between a husband and wife is to make love on a regular basis. Do not let weeks and months go by without this intimate act between the two of you. It will make him mean and frustrated, and this will only increase the tension in the home. I understand that you have a lot of other things that need your attention, such as the kids and all they are involved in, the laundry, cooking, and cleaning. I understand you may have a full-time job outside the home, as well as your ministry and other community involvement. In addition to all this, you may be working on completing your education. For a woman, there never seems to be enough time and there is always something or someone placing a demand on your time and attention. Without meaning to do so, when this happens, we usually make our husband the very last person on the list of priorities when he should be at the top, no matter what.

You must plan and organize your schedule better to make him a priority. Date nights have become very popular in our society, where you and your husband set aside a definite day and time to do something together. If this works for you, by all means, do it. If not, when he least expects it, use a vacation day and take off work, arrange for the kids to be somewhere else, cook a special meal, take a shower, use the special perfume that he really likes, put on something sexy, and then love him. For most men, this purposeful, physical intimacy changes everything. And by the way, it will bless you too!

Summary

Recognize that the tension in your home is an attack of the enemy on you, your husband, and your marriage and that you must resolve to defend your territory. How do you defend your territory?

- pray
- act like everything is all right
- forgive
- remember who you are
- remember you have the favor of God
- remember in whom you have placed your trust
- remember the victory accomplished on the cross
- remember His grace
- keep hope alive
- seek wise counsel
- fast
- get it off your brain
- communicate

- let God be God in your spouse's life
- do not neglect intimacy

The marriage union is a metaphor for the relationship between God and His people. The Word of God speaks of mutuality of love, respect, and concern between husbands and wives (Genesis 2:24, Ecclesiastes 4:9–12, Matthew 19:6, 1 Corinthians 7:3–5). Unfortunately, this does not always occur, even in Christian marriages. My discussion in this chapter is to help the spouse who is trying to live out the Word not to become bitter, frustrated, or angry, even when the other spouse doesn't seem to care. Remember: ultimately, you are only responsible for what you do or don't do. You must continue in Christlike love for your spouse and leave him or her in the hands of the Lord.

Action Item(s)

Starting today, say something encouraging to your spouse every day (even if he does not do the same for you). Encourage him in his employment. He may be facing challenges at work that he has not shared with you. If he is being considered for promotion, let him know you are pulling for him. Compliment the yard work he just completed. Thank him for washing your car and/or filling the gas tank. Compliment his recent haircut. Thank him for managing your household finances. Thank him for cooking the food even if it was burned. Tell him he's the best husband in the world (call those things that be not as though they are). You get the idea.

Do something specific to make your home more comfortable and more inviting (a sanctuary) for your spouse. For example, my husband loves for the house to smell good, so I keep plug-in air fresheners in all the outlets in my house. If he likes a certain kind of music, surprise him and have it playing when he comes home. Place a loving card or note in an unexpected place like the bathroom. Do this often enough that he begins to expect and look forward to it.

Make tonight a special evening for him (and nothing is more special to your husband than the intimacy that comes with sex). If tonight is not a good night because of his schedule, not yours, make plans for a special evening in the near future.

Prayer

Gracious God, my Father, You are the source of all that is good and right. You are not the source of the tension, distance, and strain that exists between my spouse and me. It is hard to be loving in this environment. So, Holy Spirit, as I have been forgiven, empower me to forgive any real or perceived trespasses against me by my spouse. Perfect my forgiveness concerning him/her. I need Your guidance. Revive/restore love, trust, and passion between us. Show me how to minister to and love my spouse in a manner that is gratifying to him and glorifying to You. I ask this in the precious name of Jesus. Amen!

Reflections

thrive

Chapter 5

WOMEN IN LEADERSHIP POSITIONS IN MINISTRY: THRIVING (TREADING LIGHTLY)

Our mothers and grandmothers passed down to us an oppressive heritage. They too had been oppressed. But now we must make sure our sons and daughters inherit all the promises and not allow history to repeat itself.

Bishop Jackie Green[11]

S erving in a leadership position is a call just as preaching is but for a woman, it is often quite challenging. Balancing the roles of wife, mother, preacher, career woman, and volunteer leader is going to require a great deal of proficiency, dexterity, and tough skin developed by the Holy Spirit.

As a woman in a leadership position in ministry, you will often have to say no to people who are not happy about you having the authority to approve or disapprove their requests. Some of them will silently resent you and attempt to undermine and sabotage your work, and others will openly challenge your call or leadership position. Either way, if you are in leadership as a minister or other position, you are called to serve those who support you *and* those who do not. Allow me to cite one of many examples from my personal experiences.

One Sunday after service, my husband was having a conversation with another deacon of our church. I approached my husband to tell him something, and the other deacon, out of nowhere, made a point to tell me he didn't think women should be preachers. It was as if he had been waiting for this opportunity to drop this revelation on me. A little taken aback, I simply said, "Okay," without even looking at him and directed my attention to my husband. The deacon, as if he wanted a debate, and just in case I had missed what he said, interrupted again and added, "No, no, I don't believe in women preachers. Well, maybe it's okay for women to preach but definitely not pastor."

My husband had this look on his face that said, "Brother, you are about to be told exactly what she thinks about you. You brought it on your own self." I saw my husband's look and gave him what I hoped was a reassuring smile.

Scholars have debated this issue for centuries, and I have read some of their evidence on both sides. I briefly considered calling the deacon's attention to Joel 2:28–29 (NKJV), which says,

> And it shall come to pass afterward that I will pour out My Spirit on all flesh; your sons and *your daughters shall prophesy, your old men shall dream dreams, your young men shall see visions. And also on My menservants and on My maidservants I will pour out My Spirit in those days.*

I was then going to reinforce the Old Testament endorsement of women in ministry with what Peter said in Acts 2:16–18 when he repeated Joel's prophecy. But it occurred to me this deacon probably took his position in 1 Corinthians 14:34–35 and/or 1 Timothy 2:12.

First Corinthians 14:34–35 (NKJV) says,

Let your women keep silent in the churches, for they are not permitted to speak; but they are to be submissive, as the law also says. And if they want to learn something, let them ask their own husbands at home; for it is shameful for women to speak in church.

These verses have to be dealt with in context with verses 26 and 40.

Verse 26 indicates there was a lot of activity going on in the church, and at times, too much was going on at the same time. It says, "How is it then, brethren? Whenever you come together, each of you has a psalm, has a teaching, has a tongue, has a revelation, has an interpretation. Let all things be done for edification."

Also, when we remember the cultural context of this passage, women were seated on one side of the church and men on the other side. At times, there were too many people speaking at the same time, and probably, some wives were yelling across to their husbands, asking for an explanation of certain occurrences. This interrupted the services. Paul's instruction to women to be quiet in the church was in reference to the disruption of the service. Their questions would be best addressed at home.

Also, in the early days of the church, often, services were conducted in the homes of many believers, and it was important how husbands and wives conducted themselves in the assembly of other believers. Paul addressed this issue because, apparently, it had become a problem, but it had nothing to do with whether or not women should preach. This text speaks to how husbands and wives interacted with each other in "church."

Paul is writing to the church because they were operating in chaos. *What* they were doing was good but *how* they were operating was not edifying to them. Particularly good things were being used in the wrong way; not decent and in order (verse 40).

Likewise, 1 Timothy 2:12 (KJV) addresses the interaction between husbands and wives. The text states, "But I suffer not a woman to teach, nor to usurp authority over the man, but to be in silence." I agree with this. However, if God has called a woman to preach and anointed her to operate in a specific office (pastor, prophet, teacher, ministry leader, etc.), she is not usurping authority. To usurp means to use without right or proper authorization. If God calls you, you have been authorized, sanctified, and consecrated to operate in your call, and you have a responsibility to do so.

In his book *Let Her Lead*, Brady Boyd, senior pastor of New Life Church in Colorado Springs, gives a convincing argument for women leading in ministry, citing several scholars and theologians. Boyd says, "If you are a woman called by God to lead, then *lead*. Sort out your gift-mix, scour leadership opportunities that suit your capabilities and interests, and get busy serving the body of Christ."[12]

I am appreciative of Boyd's thorough research and endorsement. However, there comes a time when, if you say you are called, you have to know that you know you are called to whatever the position is, and you don't need anyone else's approval.

In these few seconds of this encounter with the deacon, I considered engaging him in this debate. I had the thought, *Your ignorance is dazzling*, but what I said was, "Well, fortunate for us, women preachers, you don't get to make that decision. God bless you." I then spoke to my husband about what I needed to talk to him about and walked away.

I suspect that the fact that I was a preacher, coupled with the fact that I was the director of operations of our church, troubled this deacon immensely, and he wouldn't be satisfied until I knew how he felt. What he failed to realize was that I did not care not one iota what he believed. His thoughts, dogma, or philosophy were irrelevant to me. I hoped my response had conveyed that to him.

Sadly, many people in church feel this way about women preachers and women in leadership positions. Whether as a preacher, pastor, or head of a ministry, you may have opposition. Many will attempt to circumvent your authority once you make a decision. Hopefully, your pastor will not support or indulge in this kind of behavior. Nevertheless, you must strive to be gracious and loving while carrying out your ministry duties.

Another challenge I have faced as a result of being in leadership in ministry is the feeling of aloneness. As a preacher/minister (I use these terms interchangeably), there have been times I walked into a room full of male preachers, pastors, deacons, or ministry leaders and felt utterly and completely out of place, as if I shouldn't be there, as if I had invaded a secret club, as if I was not wanted and not qualified to be there. The conversation quickly changed or ceased altogether, and I felt responsible, as if I had done something wrong by walking into the room as a *woman and a minister.*

In these times, I have quickly reminded myself of the call on my life to preach and serve in the position that I held. I did not ask to preach. It was not something that, as a child, young woman, or middle-aged woman, I ever thought I would be doing. I didn't, and I don't think I'm good enough, righteous enough, smart enough, educated enough, or patient enough to be a minister/preacher. I was amazed and overwhelmed when the Lord spoke to me and said he wanted me to preach His Word! I was fifty-two years old! I was amazed and astonished that the Lord could, would use *me* to preach His glorious, good news. But once I was certain He called me, and I accepted the call, I never doubted again.

Likewise, I did not ask to hold the leadership position that I had. When my pastor initially spoke to me about serving as director of operations, I was terrified. It was a big job for which I didn't think I was qualified. Our church was in a time of tremendous growth and had recently moved onto our multimillion-dollar campus. The entire community was watching to see what we would do. Much of what had to be done rested on the guidance of the director of operations, and I did not want the responsibility of failure. Additionally, the director of operations serves on a five-member leadership council that makes all the decisions for the church. The deacon who held the position before me had done an extraordinary job and left big shoes to fill.

After my pastor and I had our initial conversation, the moment I hung up the phone, I began to talk to God. First, I just began to praise God for even being considered for such an important role in my church. My fear immediately subsided, and peace overtook me.

I was still aware that I was not the best person for the job, but the Holy Spirit gave me an assurance that I had been chosen for this time. When the pastor called me back about three weeks later, I accepted the position. I was honored to serve as director of operations for approximately two and a half years.

As a result of walking in my calling to preach and serve in leadership in my church, I realized I was even more accountable for how I treated and ministered to the people of God. In order to minister to them in a manner that they would be blessed and that God would be glorified, I discovered there were things I would have to do and not do. And so, if you are a woman in a leadership position in ministry, I make the following recommendations to you:

First, the *dos:*

- Pray, without ceasing (1 Thessalonians 5:17). You are now more of a target to the enemy than you have ever been.

- Study to show yourself approved (2 Timothy 2:15). Again, you are now more of a target to the enemy than you have ever been, and you are going to need to know the Word and have it in you.

- Encourage yourself (1 Samuel 30:6). Everybody is not going to embrace this new phase of your life.

- If you know God has called you to preach or lead in another capacity, *trust the Call.* If not sure, pray all the more and talk to your pastor.

- Do exactly what your pastor directs you to do. Don't question it except for clarification. He is responsible for guiding your calling and ministry. Remember, you represent him, your church, and the Lord.

- Be on time for everything.

- Be faithful. Show up when no one else does. But don't neglect your family. This will take skill. Remember, God established and ordained the family before He did the church.

- Develop your skills of organization and prioritizing.

- Know that your "walk" will be scrutinized more closely than it has ever been. There will be those encouraging you and praying for you. Thank them, thank God for them, and pray for them. But there will be those waiting for you to fail and fall flat on your face. Pray for them and *ignore them.*

- Be still, be quiet, be prepared, and be available. Your time to preach, teach, or organize a major function may come when you least expect it.

- Practice humility. You don't have to respond to every negative remark or attempt to injure you. You don't have to defend yourself. My grandmother used to say that if you're right, you don't have to defend yourself and that if you're wrong, you can't.

- Do your job. Do it in love. Do it in excellence, the best you can.

- Be respectful to the men and women of God who have been walking this walk for some time. You can learn something from everybody, even if it's what *not* to do, how *not* to act.

- Solicit feedback from credible sources (pastor, a mentor, other leaders, etc.).

- Make yourself accountable to someone besides your pastor, i.e., mentor, mothers, and other elders of the church. This should be someone who has demonstrated faith and excellence in their lives and has prayed for and encouraged you.

- Pray without ceasing (1 Thessalonians 5:17). You are now more of a target to the enemy than you have ever been. (I know I'm repeating myself and stating the obvious but just do it.)

Now, the *don'ts*:

- Don't take it personally when you are disrespected. This will wear you out and promote a victim's mentality.

- Don't try to call attention to what you are doing. Your work and walk will speak for themselves.

- As a preacher, never ever go into another pastor's pulpit without being invited to do so by them or directed to do so by your pastor.

- Don't look for issues. They will come to you. When they come, make a quick spiritual/mental assessment to determine if the issue requires immediate action or if it is something that will require investigation before a decision is made. This is one reason why your prayer life *must* be active and alive in order for you to make these decisions.

- Don't entertain gossip *from* anyone or *about* anyone. Doing this strips you of your credibility. When this occurs, quickly redirect the conversation into a positive direction. If the person persists, lovingly but very directly, tell them you are not going to engage in the conversation about another person. If even this fails, quickly excuse yourself.

- Don't expect to be appreciated for what you do. Just do it knowing that it is the call of God on your life.

- Don't get frustrated or angry or tired when you are not appreciated. Remember: it's the call (Galatians 6:9–10).

As I said at the beginning of this chapter, serving in a leadership position is a calling, just as preaching is. I believe that for every individual calling, the Holy Spirit gives individual direction unique to that person's call. Beginning in May 2007, before I was called to preach in February 2008, the Holy Spirit began to speak into my spirit the following words: "discipline," "obedience," "humility," and "praise." I knew this was a direction that I was supposed to apply to every area of my life. So, I attempted to do so, at home, at work, and at church. I wasn't *completely* clear as to what it meant, and thus, I wasn't sure if I was doing it right. As far as work was concerned, I was very structured, even regimented, when it came to doing my job. And so, I brought that same intensity to my spiritual development. I became more disciplined, more structured in my study time, prayer time, and fasting. I searched the Word of God and did a year-long study on humility.

At home, I became more organized in my wifely duties. Once I received and accepted my call in September 2008, this direction was reinforced and has been my marching order as to how to live and walk in my calling. It has maximized my potential and created opportunities I did not know existed.

Listen to what the Holy Spirit is saying to you and then respond accordingly. As you pray and study, He will give you a specific direction that will enable you to effectively walk in the role He has called you to.

Action Item

Identify another ministry leader who has encouraged you or given exceptional service and send a thank you note. Do this regularly, choosing a different ministry leader each time.

Actively mentor a future leader (young person) or a current leader who needs encouragement and guidance. Schedule a regular time to spend with her discussing her goals, plans, challenges, etc. Make it a regular lunch or meeting that both of you can look forward to.

Prayer

Heavenly Father, thank You for using me to serve in the area You have called me to. It is a privilege to do so. Help me not be easily offended. As I encounter challenges, disrespect, and other hurtful times, Holy Spirit, help me respond in a manner that will edify Your people and glorify You. In the precious name of Jesus, I do pray. Amen!

Reflections

thrive

Chapter 6

Thriving in Spite of Abandonment

Honoring leads to forgiveness.

Dr. Caron M. Allen

In 2017, I believed I had completed this book, having discussed what it means to be in Christ and how that knowledge is critical in thriving in all areas of one's life. The topics discussed in chapters three through five were the only topics I intended to address. As personal and difficult as these discussions were, they were nothing compared to discussing the abandonment I suffered as a child by my biological father. This was a pain that was still present, though not prevalent, as I entered my glorious sixties, and I had subconsciously pushed this pain far back into the recesses of my heart and mind. I had no intention of publicly addressing it. So, I considered the work done!

However, every time I prayed about submitting the manuscript to potential publishers, I did not get a clear sense that God was releasing me to move forward. I must admit: the first few months of being led to wait were frustrating. So, I asked, "Lord, what am I supposed to do with all this you have given me?" God's reply was "teach." And the Thriving in the Midst conference was launched in 2017.

In early 2019 I began to encounter and minister to more and more people concerning all types of abandonment but most commonly, abandonment by a spouse or father. Most of my interactions with them revealed a connection between the two. My own experience of abandonment by my biological father thrust its way back to the forefront of my mind once again. I began to go through the same steps of healing and thriving I had done in the past, and as I did so, I continued to meet more people who were struggling with this same issue.

Unexpectedly, the light bulb came on, and I realized this was the reason I had not been released to send the manuscript to a publisher. It was not complete; not until I addressed abandonment and self-care (Chapter 9).

One can feel abandoned by many different people, and the reasons are varied. In this chapter, I will only address abandonment by a parent, but I believe the steps I give you to apply will be helpful in all forms of abandonment.

"To abandon" as it relates to relationships means "to give up with the intent of never again claiming an interest in," "to withdraw from," "to withdraw protection, support, or help from." "Abandonment is the concrete, definitive action of abandoning."[13] Is this what I experienced from my biological father? Yes!

From the time I was born until the age of fourteen, I had no contact with my father despite us living in the same small town and in very close proximity to one another. There were many encounters with him or his parents, but they never acknowledged me or spoke a word to me.

Nevertheless, my grandmother always pointed them out when we encountered them and made sure I knew who they were, especially my father. As I grew older, I realized she was making sure I knew I had a father, even if he didn't act like a father, even if he didn't embrace me as his child.

At age fourteen, there was a brief outing with him that went terribly wrong, and when he took me home, my grandfather told him never to come to our home again.

Although my father was absent, I didn't lack strong, godly men in my life. I didn't miss out on a father's love. I had my great-grandfather John Burdette, my grandfathers, Riley Cain and Ralph Gibson, Sr., and my stepfather, Ralph Gibson, Jr. And then there was the *great* one, my stepfather, Phillip Hyde. I only identify him as a "step" to distinguish that we did not have the same DNA. But in every other way that mattered, he was my dad! He was a great man! They were all great men in different ways, and they all loved me and provided every material need, every emotional connection, and every practical and spiritual guidance I needed.

And yet I was still scarred from the abandonment of my biological father. I prayed for him to want me and love me. There was a gaping void in me that I did not even begin to understand until I was in my twenties, a void that only he could fill. I denied I had a need for him. I denied that his absence from my life, at times, had devastating consequences. I denied it for a long time to myself and was angry about it.

Allow me to pause here for just a minute and tell you that just as there is a place in each of our hearts that only a parent can fill, there is an even more important place reserved just for God, a place where only His love and His Spirit can fill. When you don't acknowledge this and don't ask Him in, you will always be looking for other things and people, drugs, food, sex, money, etc., to try to fill that void. But nothing else will work. Nothing and no one else can fill the space that is intended for Him!

The next time I saw my biological father was when I was twenty-nine years of age. He and his wife came to see me to apologize for his absence in my life and in an effort to establish a relationship. So, we began from that moment to try to do just that, but let me tell you: it was a challenge.

For the first year or so that we became acquainted, I kept going back in my heart and mind to his absence. I found myself contemplating a lot about how my life would have been different if he had loved me, wanted me, and been present in my life. I tried not to dwell on it, but I did. After all, it had become a habit for twenty-nine years, wondering about this man who should love me but didn't. I wanted to forgive him and move forward with a solid, loving relationship, but in my heart, I couldn't. I said I did, but I didn't. I was lost and angry, but I didn't understand who I was at that time. I only came to this realization in retrospect. And once I did, I began to be very honest with myself about the devastating consequences of his abandonment.

The time frame for this awareness was in my late thirties and early forties. It was in this same time frame that I began to study more and learn more about who I was/am in Christ, and something miraculous happened. The more I embraced my perfection (wholeness and completion) in Christ, the easier it became to face the consequences of my father's abandonment and forgive him!

I think now would be a good time to discuss some of the additional consequences I encountered because of my father's abandonment and how those consequences exhibited in my life. I want to stress again that much of the realization of the impact of my father's abandonment came during young adulthood. Even now, in my sixties, I'm still discovering how I was impacted and the negative, destructive ways in which I responded.

Consequences of Abandonment. Fear of Further Abandonment by Others

I have to say I was never afraid of being abandoned by my immediate family. My great-grandparents, maternal grandparents (who raised me), and my parents (mother and stepfather) made sure I knew I was loved and cherished. And my siblings and I were close. But outside this group of people, I was often extremely reluctant to let people get close to me. I often felt I wouldn't measure up to whatever their requirements were, and they would leave me. I remember this being most evident during my preteen and teenage years. I was timid, easily manipulated, and bullied. My friendships either didn't last long, or I tried to "buy" friends with what I had to offer. This played out very inappropriately and caused me to relinquish my virginity at an early age.

Promiscuity as a Young Woman

Fear of abandonment led to promiscuity as a young woman, which led to becoming a mother at age sixteen and then again at seventeen. Again, I only understand in retrospect that despite much love from my family, I was always needing to be embraced by others, first older girls, then boys, and then men. It was their attention that, for a short while, would make me feel good enough. But it never lasted. I quickly moved on to the next person who showed me what looked like love.

The only good that came from this desperate, reckless behavior was my two beautiful daughters. There was a fierceness lying dormant in me that was awakened at the birth of my first daughter, and by the time my second daughter was born, I began to understand that I was good enough. The proof was in God entrusting those two precious lives to me. I thrived in being a mother. I became ferocious, a lioness!

Becoming a mother, even though I wasn't much more than a child myself, changed my life for the good. And besides finding Christ, it is the best thing that has ever happened to me. This was the first personal evidence I have of God taking what the enemy meant for evil and turning it into good (Genesis 50:20). However, the insecurities continued for quite some time.

Shame

Abandonment caused me to be ashamed when I was growing up. Everyone in my small hometown knew who my father was and knew he wanted nothing to do with me. I was harshly ridiculed by my peers. Even though financially, my grandparents and parents took very good care of me, abandonment was my one weakness. I was ashamed my father didn't love me, and the shame led to self-loathing.

Self-Loathing

For years I waivered back and forth about who I was; if I was pretty enough, smart enough, or good enough. I already had much proof that I was "enough," but the nagging question would often arise within me, "Well, why doesn't my father love me? I must be bad, ugly, and stupid." For years, I thought nothing good would happen to me. I knew this was not true because I had my daughters. But self-loathing will cause you to ignore the obvious truths and search for the lies.

Self-loathing can be so terribly detrimental, and you must be intentional and consistent in speaking the truth of who you are in Christ over yourself. I make declarations daily about who I am in the Lord. Among others, I confirm these truths from Ephesians 1:2–14. I am:

- a recipient of grace and peace

- blessed

- chosen

- holy

- blameless

- predestined

- adopted

- accepted

- redeemed

- forgiven

- informed

- enlightened

- given revelation

- legitimate

- recipient of an inheritance (legacy)

- the praise of His glory

- wise

- sealed

Isolation and Loneliness

Before I began my journey of learning more about who I am in Christ, the shame and self-loathing of abandonment led to isolation and loneliness. Again, this was most prevalent in my youth. I felt alone and wouldn't tell my grandparents how I felt because I didn't know how to say it. I didn't understand it at that time. As I grew into my teens and young adulthood, I was often accused of being stuck up, aloof, snobbish, and having other less flattering traits. So, I tried to be friendly, but most times, I tried too hard. This led to further rejection. I was awkward and very unpopular. Becoming a mother changed most of my feelings about myself for the better, but every now and then, I would slip back into the "woe is me" attitude.

Hard-Heartedness

As a teenager and young adult, abandonment caused me to try to act tougher than I was. I developed a "fake" thick skin. I endeavored to give the appearance that I didn't care whether I was liked by my peers. Even after I began to know the truth of who I am in Christ, I would still, on occasion, put up an invisible wall, thinking I had to protect myself from further abandonment. Vulnerability was not an option. It has taken years for me not to be afraid to be open and available to love others as Christ does. And it is an ongoing process.

Inability to Trust

The abandonment and my responses to it negatively impacted many other relationships. I worked hard at keeping people at a distance. When I did let people get close, it was a slow, sometimes agonizing process. To say I had trust issues would be an understatement. I wanted to love and be loved; I wanted to be friendly and have real friends. It was just too much work for someone who was so insecure and trying hard not to let it show.

Confusion

This led to much confusion within, which caused me to focus even more on my father's rejection. It made no sense to me. I was always asking myself, "Why doesn't my father love me?" "What's was wrong with me?" So, to negate his absence and lack of love for me, I tried to prove I was lovable by looking for love from men.

Anger

There were many mistakes, bad choices, and wrong decisions, coupled with the above-mentioned negative responses, that caused me to be very angry, especially as a teenager. I hated my father for what he had done to me. Yet, I longed for his love and acknowledgment. I hated myself for allowing his absence to impact me so devastatingly. Despite an entire "village" of other wonderful people who loved, nurtured, and cherished me, I was in turmoil.

How do we thrive in spite of abandonment?

When my father finally contacted me, for a time, it heightened my anger and fear. I didn't know how to respond to his efforts to connect. I was never rude or impertinent, but I was distant and cold toward him. I acted in a manner that would make him think I didn't need him, that I didn't care whether he wanted me or not, that I didn't care that he was sorry for abandoning me. But slowly, over time, I realized my pretenses were creating further harm to myself and possibly my daughters. I prayed for guidance. I talked to my grandmother, and her words were profound. She said, "Be respectful." And in my inner being, I heard, "Honor your father." But how do you honor someone who has ignored your very existence? How do you honor someone who has done nothing to care for or protect you?

I went to the Word of God and found this mandate in Exodus 20:12 and in Deuteronomy 5:16 (NKJV): "Honor your father and your mother, as the Lord your God has commanded you, that your days may be long, and that it may be well with you in the land which the Lord your God is giving you."

The one thing I was intentional in doing was to honor him. Being completely honest, I can say I never grew to love him as a father, but I honored him according to the word of God. And honoring led to forgiveness. Honoring him softened my heart and made me receptive to his attempt to connect.

How do you honor your parent when they have abandoned you?

- Visit in person, if feasible. If not…

- Communicate (call or write)

- Be honest with him/her about how you feel, *IF* you can do so in a respectful manner; if not, wait until you can.

- Acknowledge who they are. Don't pretend they don't exist.

- Be courteous to them.

- Speak respectfully concerning him/her, or don't speak at all. Matthew 15:4 (NKJV) cautions us, "For God commanded, saying, 'Honor your father and your mother'; and 'He who curses father or mother, let him be put to death.'" You can be brutally honest with your counselor about the impact of his/her absence from your life but don't use this patient/client privilege to purposely degrade them.

- Allow them to bless you but not buy you.

- Forgive! Honoring leads to forgiveness.

- Ask the Holy Spirit for help. It may be a slow and initially painful process, but you can do all things through Christ, even honoring a parent who has abandoned you.

Action Item(s)

The following actions are steps I have taken to help me honor, forgive, and heal from abandonment:

- seek counseling,

- don't pretend there is no pain,

- ask the Holy Spirit for guidance.

Prayer

Dear Lord, help me deal with the abandonment I've suffered in a godly way. Help me forgive those who have hurt me. Help me honor and bless them according to Your will. In Jesus's name, I pray. Amen!

Reflections

thrive

When the Enemy Comes in like a Flood

So shall they fear the name of the Lord from the west, and His glory from the rising of the sun; when the enemy comes in like a flood, the Spirit of the Lord will lift up a standard against him.

Isaiah 59:19 (NKJV)

*N*avigating your way through any one of the aforementioned situations (challenging work environment, tension-filled home, ministry leadership, and abandonment) is challenging, but oftentimes, the enemy of the saints will attack you in more than one area at the same time. You feel surrounded by the enemy present on every hand. You find yourself struggling at work, at home, at church, in extended family relationships, in your health, the health of loved ones, and in your finances, just to name a few. Peace, contentment, joy, and fulfillment cannot be found anywhere. *This is the enemy coming in like a flood*, and this continues to be his preferred plan of attack, at least for me. But the last portion of Isaiah

59:19 tells us that when the enemy does bombard you on every side, the Holy Spirit raises a standard, a defense against him.

I have come to understand that Christ is the "standard." His death on the cross and resurrection from the dead set us free from sin and death once we accept Him as Savior. Galatians 2:20 (NKJV) says, "I have been crucified with Christ; it is no longer I who live, but Christ lives in me; and the life which I now live in the flesh I live by faith in the Son of God, who loved me and gave Himself for me."

The life we live in the flesh is a walk of faith. This walk includes the challenges I have discussed in this work, as well as numerous others. We are victorious in this walk with Christ as the standard. He is our perfect example of how to engage the enemy, and when we respond appropriately, we lift Him up!

In 1 Thessalonians 5:16–22 (NKJV), Paul outlines a detailed seven-step plan for responding to the enemy's attack. He writes:

> Rejoice always, pray without ceasing, in everything give thanks; for this is the will of God in Christ Jesus for you. Do not quench the Spirit. Do not despise prophecies. Test all things; hold fast what is good. Abstain from every form of evil.

In this epistle to the church in Thessalonica, Paul is encouraging this group of new believers to stand strong. The Thessalonian believers had a lot going against them. Intense persecution from outside the church, false teachers within the church, and sexual immorality among themselves were just a few of their struggles. Nevertheless, Paul was encouraged by the report Timothy gave him concerning them because they had demonstrated faith and love for each other, for Paul, and for the Lord. They were trying to hold on and do what was pleasing in the eyes of the Lord, but the attack against them was constant and fierce. They needed guidance.

In this last chapter of Paul's first letter to this church, he identifies seven steps for not just surviving trials but for living victoriously despite the trials. When we look at this Scripture and then read any one of the four Gospel accounts of Jesus's life, we see this is how Jesus lived His life. Therefore, Paul's instructions to the Thessalonians are a perfect plan for us as we, too, are often bombarded on every side.

Rejoice Always

First, Paul tells us to *rejoice!* Really? *Yes!* On first consideration, when you read this direction, it seems irrational. You may ask yourself, "How can I rejoice when I'm under attack at work, my husband and I are not getting along, my kids are acting crazy, my mother is sick?" and on and on and on.

What Paul is telling us here is to rejoice, not in our present circumstances, not for what we are going through right now, but to rejoice in the hope we have in Christ. Rejoice in your knowledge that God can and will work all things for your good.

We do not serve an uncaring, aloof, remote, unfeeling, distant, deity. No! Hebrews 4:15 (NKJV) tells us, "For we do not have a high priest who is unable to empathize with our weaknesses, but we have one who has been tempted in every way, just as we are—yet He did not sin." He identifies with our pain, our fears, our disappointments, and our discouragement. He was touched by the feeling of our infirmities at all points. He understands. He sees you right where you are. He knows what you're going through. He knows how you are feeling. He knows. He cares. He hears. He is uniquely qualified to be our standard. This is what we take joy in.

Another reason to rejoice is because there are benefits to your tribulations (trials, pressures, suffering). It will not feel good, but when you respond in the knowledge of Christ and who you are in Him, tribulations produce perseverance; perseverance produces character, and character produces hope (Romans 5:3–5).

The Greek word Paul used for character refers to metal purified of dross. The *Merriam-Webster Collegiate Dictionary* defines "dross" as "the scum that forms on the surface of molten metal; waste or foreign matter; impurity; something that is base, trivial, or inferior."[14] Rejoice because the pressure caused by your struggles will work the junk and impurities out of you. We must go through the fires of purification in order for our true potential to be revealed.

Rejoice because it is in the adversities of life that God becomes more real and more personal to us. When we respond appropriately, it is in the adversities of life that God is magnified, made bigger in our view of Him. He does not get any bigger. He is already omnipotent (all-powerful), omniscient (all-knowing), and omnipresent (everywhere at the same time). But praising Him helps us to see Him better, and thus, He looks bigger to us. To magnify Him is to make Him bigger than your situation.

During a three-month period in 2015, the flood coming against me consisted of, in part, several family members estranged from one another, physical fights, two diagnoses of cancer in my family (lung and breast), a severe stroke that rendered a family member blind and paralyzed on one side of the body, another family member tried to hurt themself, one daughter and granddaughter were in a car accident that totaled the vehicle, marriages in trouble, relapse of multiple sclerosis, and three deaths. This was not the first time in my life that I had dealt with a multitude of crises, and fortunately, I knew exactly what to do. I began to pray and rejoice in the Lord. My initial rejoicing was something like this: "Okay, Lord, this all looks really crazy, but I praise You anyhow. I will not fall apart or succumb to fear or worry. You are worthy to be praised, no matter what. I trust You, Lord. My life is in Your hands. The lives of my family members are in Your hands. I give You glory, Lord. I adore You, God. You are awesome forever. Heal, deliver, restore, set free in the name of Jesus, I pray. Amen!"

Some days my praise was more enthusiastic than on other days. Some days I did not feel like praising. Those were the times I had to make myself praise based on what I knew about God and not on how I felt. Sometimes I had to remind myself to rejoice in the Lord always. Again, I say, rejoice (Philippians 4:4).

As a result of this specific attack, my family and I instituted a weekly prayer meeting by way of a phone conference. We were calling in from Colorado, Georgia, Michigan, Florida, and Arizona. We have continued this practice for the past seven years. It has been amazing to watch how God has moved in all of our circumstances!

Pray without Ceasing

Next, Paul tells us to pray without ceasing. Praying is communicating with God, talking to Him, and listening to Him. To pray without ceasing is to be in a constant state of awareness that God is always with you, and no matter what situation you find yourself in, He is there in it with you. He is a very present help, especially in a time of trouble (Psalm 46:1). No matter how big or small the trouble might be, you must talk to God about it.

To pray without ceasing is to be aware that He is here with you, and you must talk to Him about all things at all times, sometimes out loud, sometimes quietly. To pray without ceasing is to seek Him in all decisions, major and minor, realizing nothing concerning you is unimportant to Him.

Praying without ceasing does not mean to always be making your requests known to God but sometimes *thanking* Him for the moment, *thanking* Him for the direction you just received, *thanking* Him for *being able* to do whatever you need Him to do, even if He doesn't do it, *thanking* Him for the knowledge that He is with you, *thanking* Him for just being God.

When praying, spend some time being quiet and listening for Him to speak. Remember: praying is a conversation between you and God, and any effective conversation must contain speaking and listening.

Write Your Prayer Down

Since 2008, I have made it a practice to write my prayer down to bring structure and focus to my prayer time. Although it's written down, I pray it out loud. My prayer is detailed and precise, so I don't miss anything I had intended to pray for. This is especially helpful when dealing with several different issues at the same time. This prayer has evolved over the years as the Holy Spirit has given revelation and answers.

I consider my written prayer as my battle plan. No general goes into battle without a well-thought-out plan. Writing my prayer down helps me organize my thoughts, and I can more easily identify answers when they come. Although my prayer is written down, I remain open to the Holy Spirit, and when He leads in another direction, I follow. For instance, sometimes I open up my written down prayer, and He tells me to pray in my Spirit language, in tongues. Sometimes I start to pray, and He says to just read and pray the Word. Sometimes, I start to pray, and all I do is praise and worship.

Prayer will equip you to respond to the challenges of life by displaying the fruit of the Spirit as outlined in Galatians 5:22–24: love, joy, peace, long-suffering, kindness, goodness, faithfulness, gentleness, and self-control. These Godly attributes will be evident as you continue to walk in the knowledge of who you are in the Lord. Allow me to explain.

In circumstances where you don't feel loved, you demonstrate *love* nevertheless, even to the one who has hurt you. You continue to do the pleasing, loving things you always did.

When your feelings have been hurt and you are sad or lonely, you will find *joy* in the Lord by reading the Word, praising and worshiping, remembering past victories, and remembering God's faithfulness. You also can find joy by blessing others or by doing those things you enjoy, such as a trip to the spa, the movies, the library, or an afternoon of tea at a local tea house.

During chaotic circumstances and everybody else is falling apart, you will have divine *peace*. Additionally, you will excel in doing your part to maintain peace. You will not always feel you have to be heard. You will know when to speak and when to be silent.

An effective, fervent prayer life will reveal to you the areas where the Lord has demonstrated great grace and mercy toward you. You will, in turn, become more patient and *long-suffering* with others. You will not have to pray for patience; it is a byproduct, a consequence of praying and walking in love.

You will respond to acts of sabotage and treachery with *kindness*, such as praying for the offender, helping them with an issue, and ministering to them in whatever fashion they may need.

Prayer will cause you to look for opportunities to do *good*, such as participating in or giving to a charity. Despite how you are treated, you will treat people right because it is the right thing to do, even if they don't respond in kind. Whenever I think someone has intentionally said or done something to injure me, I have made it a practice that I intentionally respond by doing something positive. Sometimes I do something for the person, and sometimes, I don't. It just depends on what becomes the first opportunity I have. I act immediately if I can. This takes my mind off the offense and allows God to use me to bless someone.

Faithfulness is demonstrated when you maintain your upright walk and continue to witness to, encourage, and bless others.

A consistent prayer life will facilitate a confident, calm, gentle demeanor. You will display *gentleness* in the most trying circumstances and to the harshest, rudest people. Proverbs 25:15 tells us a gentle tongue breaks a bone and 1 Peter 3:4 tells us a gentle spirit is precious in the sight of God.

Instead of going off and being rude to someone who is rude to you, you demonstrate *self-control*. Your self-control will leave them puzzled and may present an opportunity for you to witness to them about the love of God.

I am not saying this is going to be easy. As a matter of fact, at times, it will be extremely difficult. This is something you do on purpose, reminding yourself in chaos and trials to demonstrate the fruit of the Spirit and not respond to what your flesh wants. Paul calls this crucifying the flesh. By doing what is right according to the Word and will of God and not doing what you *feel* like doing, you put your flesh under submission, and God is glorified!

In Everything, Give Thanks, for This Is the Will of God in Christ Jesus for You

This directive tells us that while in the midst of life's challenges and trials, we are to give thanks. Why? In doing so, we demonstrate our trust in the Lord. We demonstrate we will not be overcome by the circumstances. We demonstrate that we know God is in control and working things for our good. Most importantly, it is His will that we give thanks.

Do Not Quench the Spirit

To disobey these admonishments in this text (and others) is not to allow the Holy Spirit to have His complete work in your life. Quenching the Holy Spirit results in a decrease of the anointing in your life. If you are challenged in displaying any of this fruit, ask the Holy Spirit to empower and enable you to do so. Your request releases His full power in your life.

Do Not Despise Prophecies

Prophetic revelations, instructions, or warnings you receive through your pastor or other credible sources should be appreciated and given full consideration. We are to recognize the value of this gift (1 Corinthians 14:3).

Test All Things; Hold Fast What Is Good

When prophecies are given, or anything that is said to be *of* the Lord or *from* the Lord, it should be put to the test. And the test is this: Is it scriptural? How do you determine if it is scriptural?

You have to know and continue to study the Word. Conduct topical research. Use your concordance. Compare various translations. Study other resources, such as commentaries. If what you have been told lines up with Scripture, receive it and apply it to your life.

Abstain from Every Form of Evil

If what you have been told does not line up with Scripture, reject it. To abstain from evil means to walk in the way of the Lord. Do not give in to the desires of the flesh. Do not do what you feel like doing. And don't associate with those who do.

I don't believe it is a coincidence that there are seven directives in this process. Seven is the number of completion, and if we follow Paul's guidance in this scripture, we will thrive and find peace, even when challenged in more than one area at the same time.

Summary

The first chapter of this book talks about the new you in Christ. You must remember you are being changed, taught, tempered, prepared, and placed back on the potter's wheel (Jeremiah 18:3–4). It will be trying at times, but you were created for this. These light and momentary afflictions (2 Corinthians 4:17) are temporary. They are meant for your *instruction* and not your *destruction*. It is needed for you to reach your expected end. So, when the going gets tough, and it will get tough, *having done all*, all the things we have talked about in this book (prayer, remembering, hoping, fasting, praising, journaling, trusting God, etc.), *stand*.

In Ephesians 6:10–18, Paul gives us specific instructions on how to stand outfitted, equipped in the full armor of God.

The belt of truth (verse 14) (see also Psalm 51:6):

As Paul was writing about weapons of warfare, he considered how the Roman soldier was outfitted for battle. First, a soldier put on a tunic that covered him from about neck to thigh. The tunic was secured around the waist with a belt that allowed him to fight unencumbered. As it relates to spiritual warfare, the abdomen area was generally thought to be the area of emotions. To bind this area with truth is to command your emotions to believe the truth of the Word of God. Our tunic or covering is Jesus Christ. The belt is the truth of the cross, Christ's resurrection, and His ascension. The knowledge of this truth enables us to live a life of honesty and integrity, causing us to be one in purpose with Christ, who is the *truth*, according to John 14:6.

How do you effectively "put on" the belt of truth? You do so by committing to live right and righteously before God, trusting in the Holy Spirit and His Word to guide you. This requires consistent time in prayer, as well as reading, studying, and meditating on His Word.

The breastplate of righteousness (verse 14) (see also Psalm 5:12; 2 Corinthians 6:7):

The breastplate of the Roman soldier covered him from neck to thigh, protecting the heart and chest cavity. Spiritually, the heart must be shielded from sin to prevent unrighteousness from settling within. This can only be done by confessing one's sin and receiving forgiveness based on the shedding of the blood of Christ on the cross (1 John 1:9). The breastplate of the righteousness of Christ puts us in right standing with God. We don't have to seek protection or right standing through our works. Jesus paid it all. We can stand confidently in Him.

We must know with certainty that the righteousness of Christ is applied to us once we accept Him as Savior. Isaiah 61:10 (NKJV) says,

> I will greatly rejoice in the Lord, my soul shall be joyful in my God; for He has clothed me with the garments of salvation, He has covered me with the robe of righteousness, as a bridegroom decks himself with ornaments, and as a bride adorns herself with her jewels.

The various forms of the Hebrew and Greek word for "cover" or "covering" (*kasha, haphah, kesut, kalypto, epikalypto,* etc.) indicate a greater degree of protection. The righteousness of Christ is a breastplate that hides or conceals or covers our sin from God's view. This is what forgiveness is. His righteousness also covers or protects us from the devices and tricks of the enemy. Hallelujah!

How do you effectively apply the righteousness of Christ? We must know this and speak this to the enemy when he comes against us by trying to make us doubt the effectiveness of the righteousness of Christ and doubt that we have His righteousness applied to us. First Corinthians 1:30 (NKJV) says, "But of Him you are in Christ Jesus, who became for us wisdom from God—and *righteousness* and sanctification and redemption—that, as it is written, 'He who glories, let him glory in the Lord.'"

Second Corinthians 5:21 (NKJV) says, "For He made Him who knew no sin to be sin for us, that we might become the *righteousness* of God in Him."

The gospel of peace (verse 15) (see also Isaiah 52:7, Philippians 4:7):

As Paul continued to have in mind the Roman soldiers' outfitting for battle, he considered how they protected their feet. Soldiers wore sandals that had sharp cleats that dug into the ground, giving them firm footing and enabling them to walk on very rough, uneven terrain.

Spiritually, preparation speaks to a prepared foundation that consists of the gospel (good news) of peace with God (Ephesians

2:17). This peace that surpasses all understanding will definitely be needed when in a challenging, tense environment. This peace will keep you calm and serene, no matter what is happening around you, no matter what the enemy is saying to you. The truth of the Word and the Holy Spirit in you will keep you and allow you to withstand as you encounter strongholds. You will find you are not easily shaken by the challenges of life that the enemy will throw at you.

Because your spiritual "feet" (your foundation) are prepared in the gospel of the peace received from God, your "footing" is as sure as that of the deer that walks on high, rocky, mountainous trails (Habakkuk 3:19). You will be able to "walk" above the noise and distractions of your environment. Additionally, preparing ourselves with this Gospel of peace signifies our readiness to share the good news of Jesus with others at a moment's notice.

How do we effectively use the gospel of peace? Remember: just look back over your life and remember past situations where you were challenged but came out victorious. Read Lamentations 3:22–24. Your peace will be in the knowledge of God's faithfulness toward you.

The shield of faith (verse 16) (see also Hebrews 10:38; 11:6):

The Roman soldier carried a long, oblong-shaped barrier that was covered with wood or animal hides and bound together by iron. When soaked in water, the fiery arrows of the enemy could not penetrate this shield. And when soldiers fought close together, side by side, they gave each other added protection from the enemy.

What Christ accomplished on the cross is the object of our faith, which is the only faith God recognizes and the only faith Satan recognizes. The faith of the cross will empower you to receive and believe and embrace that which you do not yet fully comprehend. The faith in the cross serves as an impenetrable barrier between you and the temptation Satan throws at you, the temptation of the flesh and mind. The shield of faith gives you access to God's boundless power and wisdom and enables you to resist the fiery darts of distressing circumstances and temptations to do evil.

How do we effectively use the shield of faith? Speaking, by faith, the Word of God, when confronted by strongholds or arguments, is an effective weapon. Also, uniting your faith with other believers offers additional support. A three-strand cord is not easily broken (Ecclesiastes 4:12). When one is lacking, the other holds her up. If my faith is wavering, her "shield" of faith helps cover me and vice versa.

The helmet of salvation (verse 17) (see also 1 Thessalonians 5:8; Isaiah 59:17):

A soldier's helmet was made of bronze and had leather attachments to hold it firmly in place.

The helmet represents the head and mind and also has to do with the renewing of the mind. This is done by understanding and reminding ourselves that everything we receive from the Lord comes to us through the Cross.

Our salvation is sure and gives us protection from the enemy's attacks (1 John 5:11–13). Because of salvation, we are delivered from sin and its impact on our lives, we have the guarantee of future eternal deliverance from every kind of evil, and God continues the work of sanctification in our lives.

The certainty of your salvation, the knowledge that you are sanctified, protected, delivered from sin and temptation, and covered by the blood of Christ, will empower you to stand confidently in a challenging environment.

How do you effectively apply the helmet of salvation? You do so by remembering who you were before salvation and afterward. You can recite or read the scriptures that speak to how we accept Christ (see Romans 3:23; 5:8; 6:23; 10:9–13).

The sword of the spirit, which is the Word of God (verse 17) (see also Revelation 1:16):

The sword is the only offensive weapon identified in this arsenal. It's the only weapon that has to be used. All the other weapons are effective simply by being present. However, the sword has to be wielded, utilized, and put into action. When Paul identifies the sword as the Word of God, he refers to specific sections of Scripture that the Holy Spirit will bring to mind to meet a particular need. One example is when Jesus used specific sections of Deuteronomy in His encounter with Satan in the desert (Luke 4:1–13).

How do we effectively use this weapon of the Word of God? We do so by reading, studying, memorizing, meditating on, speaking, and living this Word.

Prayer (verse 18) (see also James 5:16; Matthew 26:41; 1 Thessalonians 5:17, 25):

Prayer concludes the weapons of our warfare identified in chapter 6 of Ephesians. Prayer must be constant for us to be effective in pursuing excellence in all areas of our lives. Prayer should be a regular part of your life before a crisis occurs. Thus, when we encounter challenging situations, prayer will be automatic, your default position.

Prayer is the communication between you and God. Prayer is how we receive commands and encouragement for the battle. We must be in constant communication with our Father.

How do we effectively use this weapon of prayer? Simply by doing it! Pray alone or with a prayer partner! Our prayers for one another are powerful (James 5:16). Pray corporately. Pray anytime, in all things. Pray all kinds of prayers; short prayers, in-depth prayers; scripture prayers! *Just pray!*

Additional Weapons of Warfare

The Lord Jesus Christ (Romans 13:11–14):

Another effective weapon of warfare is the knowledge of having the Lord Jesus Christ on your side. He is our divine advocate. He sits at the right hand of our Father, interceding on our behalf (Romans 8:34; Hebrews 7:25).

In Romans 13:11–14, Paul is encouraging the early Christians, as well as us today, to be watchful and aware of the second coming of Christ. Because this second coming is inevitable, there will be constant attacks by the enemy to try to derail as many people as possible. As Christians, we should live daily for Christ. And therein lies the battle.

"Putting on Christ" means living like Him, loving like Him, remembering the victory he accomplished for us at the cross, and receiving His grace! When we do this in the midst of a tough situation, we thrive.

The glory of God is my rearguard (Isaiah 58:8):

In verses 1–5 of chapter 58, the prophet Isaiah was telling the people of Israel that the reason their fasting was unproductive was because they were fasting for the wrong reasons. They sought their own pleasure in fasting, oppressed their slaves while fasting, and quarreled and fought while fasting. Their fasting did not draw them closer to God and, therefore, was a waste of time. However, Isaiah encouraged them that once they began to fast with a true desire to serve God and with a greater awareness of the judgment, mercy, and faith of God, they would experience a closer walk with God.

Another reward of fasting would be the glory of the Lord protecting them from the rear, not allowing any unexpected attacks or ambushes from the enemy. Likewise, for us today, as we take our stand against the enemy in a challenging situation, we are unable to see from all angles, from all sides. But God sees what's in front of us, what's behind us, and what we're dealing with right now. He has us covered from every possible avenue of attack, even the rear.

How do we effectively use this weapon of the glory of God being our rearguard?

We don't have to do anything but remind ourselves that the glory of God has our back.

The joy of the Lord is my strength (Nehemiah 8:10):

Nehemiah, while in exile, had risen to high office in the Persian Empire, serving as "cupbearer" or personal advisor to King Artaxerxes. Nehemiah was concerned that the walls of Jerusalem were in ruin, and he believed he was the one to motivate the people to rebuild them. Through a series of miraculous events, King Artaxerxes allowed Nehemiah to move to Jerusalem and provided the means and protection necessary to rebuild the city's defenses. The favor of God is a wondrous thing!

Once the wall was rebuilt and many of the people returned to Jerusalem, they celebrated the Feast of the Trumpets. As part of the celebration, the Law was read out loud in Hebrew and interpreted in Aramaic. The reading and receiving of the law was a joyous time, but when the people heard the law and realized how disobedient they had been, they wept. This was when Nehemiah told them to "go your way, eat the fat, drink the sweet, and send portions to those for whom nothing is prepared; for this day is holy to our Lord. Do not sorrow, *for the joy of the Lord is your strength*" (Nehemiah 8:10, NKJV).

The people were encouraged to rejoice because God was rejoicing in them. The joy spoken of here is the joy that filled God's heart because of their obedience, which meant both strength and safety to them. If we follow their example, we, too, will experience the joy of the Lord, and it will be our strength during all challenging times. Remember: this is God's joy that we are privileged to share. We take our rest in our knowledge of who He is and who we are in Him.

Consequently, this gives us peace, joy, and assurance in the best and the worst of times.

How do we apply the joy of the Lord? As you maintain your witness for the Lord and navigate your way through treacherous circumstances, remember in whom you have placed your trust. This remembering will allow you to thrive in an environment that is deadly to others.

As you take your position of steadfast trust in the Lord, consider the following:

- Never try to predetermine or predict whom God will use to minister to you. It could be the least expected person. It may be someone you don't even know, but they will be well prepared to speak to you because of their experience or what the Lord has revealed to them.

- When you don't hear from God, trust Him. When you see no difference in your situation, trust Him.

- Cast all your care upon Him, for He cares for you (1 Peter 5:7). How do you cast your care? Every time the enemy tells you something contrary to the Word of God, you must audibly speak the truth to him. Every time the enemy reminds you of a past sin or mistake, you must audibly remind him that you have been forgiven and now walking in the will of the Lord. Every time the enemy tells you you're nothing, tell him who you are in Christ. No matter how often you have to do it, *do it*! Even if it's every few minutes. When the enemy talks to you about you, you talk to him about God. That might be something like this: "Satan, I have been forgiven for that. God loves me. Christ redeemed me, and now I am the righteousness of Him. I am perfect (whole and complete) in Him, and I will be and do all He has called me to be and do. His grace toward me was not in vain."

143

When you start to worry, stop, and pray. Talk to the Lord about it. Tell Him why you are worried. Ask the Holy Spirit to help you fully release the issue to Him. Spend time being silent and listening for direction.

When you start to worry about a specific issue, apply the Word to that issue. If you don't know any Scripture that would be relevant, look for one. Use your concordance to do a topical search. Most study Bibles have designated sections dedicated to current relevant topics of concern.

When worry attacks your heart and mind, do something! You have to practice casting to get good at it!

The second part of 1 Peter 5:7 (NKJV) says, "[…] for He cares for you." The Greek word for care used in this verse is *melei*, which means "to have a compassionate interest in." You are His concern. God the Father has proven His interest in us and His love for us by giving His only Son to die for us. God the Son has demonstrated His care for us by giving up His place in glory to take on mortal flesh and be subjected to all that flesh has to contend with, and yet, He did not sin. God, the Holy Spirit, demonstrates His care for us, His compassionate interest in us by being our *Paraclete*, our helper, our advocate, our counselor, and our comforter.

When you don't know what else or what different thing to do, keep doing what you know to do (praying, reading the Word, fasting, etc.). The enemy will try to convince you that it does no good, that it's not working, and that it's a waste of time. *Ignore* him!

Get up early to talk to the Lord (Mark 1:35). It was on many days when I got up early that the Lord gave me a word of hope, instruction, or encouragement. I am not a morning person, and getting up early is hard for me, but most times, when I do, I hear from the Lord.

Stay humble but don't act like a victim. Walk in the knowledge that you are victorious in the Lord (2 Corinthians 2:14).

Be happy as you rest in the supremacy of God's love for you. I'm not talking about a false happiness, where you are pretending nothing is wrong. I am referring to a real commitment to rest in the joy of the Lord; rest in your knowledge that He has everything under control and working all things for your good. I'm talking about a divine confidence in whom He is and who you are in Him. You can, and you should enjoy your life right in the midst of all your challenges. It's okay to have joy even when problems are occurring. This demonstrates your faith in God. Defy the enemy; confuse the enemy; frustrate the enemy. How? Be happy!

Suddenly

God is working in your situation, and your breakthrough could come suddenly on a regular day. There will come a definitive moment of clarity and illumination, like when Peter saw the angel who appeared to him in prison. Acts 12:7 says a light shone. It happened to me, and that light blinded out some things and revealed others.

It could be a regular day when you hear Him as you have never heard Him before, and what He says will change everything.

It happened to me on March 1, 2013. To me, He simply said, "It's working for your good." I had heard this a hundred times before, either in a song or from some well-meaning person attempting to encourage me. I had read it in His Word (Romans 8:28) and even spoken it to myself numerous times. But at this moment, when God spoke it to me, I almost collapsed to the floor. It was more than speaking; it was a *revelation* through the presence of the Lord. He was there, and His presence was a brightness exploding inside of my soul, spirit, and body. It was a moment of such brilliance and epic significance that my knees buckled, and I had to take hold of the bed to keep from falling. I was breathless!

It was a moment when I received a blessed assurance; a moment when the light and love of the Lord's glory illuminated my heart with such radiance and vividness and exposed every dark, obscure, dry, broken, fragmented, bitter, desperate, confused, frantic aspect of my life. I saw it all, at that moment, and for the first time, I was not afraid to look at it, all the secret hurt and pain, those things I had never told anybody, those things buried deep within my heart and conscience, all the sin and ugliness that I had done or had been done to me. I looked at it all with no fear, no trepidation, or condemnation as I heard the Holy Spirit simply say, "It's working for your good."

It was a moment of clarity, certainty, and conviction. In that moment, I began to worship Him for allowing me to see and understand like never before. I began to cry tears of joy as all doubt and fear washed from my soul, and in its place was peace and assurance that it *is* working for my good. So simple yet so profound!

Now I know and have come to understand much better what happened to Saul (Paul) when the Lord spoke to him on the Damascus Road (Acts 9:3–8). It all became clear: the reading, the praying, and the speaking by faith. The Lord manifested it into revelation.

I wish I could describe it better. I pray I can help you to understand that God is working in your situation. You may have been waiting on a word from the Lord, maybe for what seems like a long time. I understand. I've been there when I reached the end of my rope and wanted to *give up*. But the knowledge of the Great I Am caused me to *get up*.

I've been there, paralyzed in fear, in the midst of my gifts and challenges, wondering if God would or could make anything good out of the mess I had created. Then suddenly, that still small voice reminded me that He who is in me is greater than he who is in the world (1 John 4:4). Suddenly, that still small voice reminded me that I could come boldly to the throne of grace where all fear must subside (Hebrews 4:16). Quietly, He whispered to my soul, "It's working for your good," and my heart soared in thankfulness!

I say to you: you can thrive in every situation. In addition to what we have already discussed in this work, Paul sums it up very succinctly in his second epistle to Timothy 4:5 (NKJV). He says to the young pastor and to us today, "[Y]ou be watchful in all things, endure afflictions, do the work of an evangelist, fulfill your ministry."

Paul gives this directive with military curtness and authority. He forcefully uses these action words: "be," "endure," "do," and "fulfill." It is not a request; it is a command for his son in the ministry and for us.

In my spirit, this command was translated into, "Suck it up, stop whining, don't panic; you were built for this! Be disciplined, be obedient, and be humble in your life. Be diligent in living a godly life. Do the work you are called to do, which is leading others to Christ." And when you do this, 1 Peter 5:10 (NKJV) tells us,

> [...] the God of all grace, who called us to His eternal glory by Christ Jesus, after you have suffered a while, will perfect, establish, strengthen, and settle you. To Him be the glory and the dominion forever and ever. Amen.

Hallelujah! Thank You, Jesus!

When the enemy comes in like a flood, remember: Jesus is the standard, and He has equipped you with powerful weapons to stand against the enemy.

Action Item

Today, focus on past victories. As you begin to remember, write them down to refer to later. If you can't think of anything, check your journal.

Prayer

Heavenly Father, I come boldly before Your throne, and I acknowledge the enormity of the challenges in my life. I remind myself that You are the God of all grace and that whatever You allow is working for my good. With this knowledge, O Lord, I declare I can do all things through Christ who strengthens me. Thank You, Holy Spirit, for reminding me that He who began a good work in me will see it to completion, and the trials of life will not overwhelm me as long as I depend on You and not my own strength. Father, I confess that I get tired, both physically and spiritually. I confess that I get confused and often don't know what to do. Holy Spirit, empower me to trust in You with all my heart and lean not on my own understanding. I need You, Lord; I can't do anything without You. In Jesus's name, I pray. Amen!

Reflections

thrive

Chapter 8

RESTING IN HIS LOVE

On the same day, when evening had come, He said to them, "Let us cross over to the other side." Now when they had left the multitude, they took Him along in the boat as He was. And other little boats were also with Him. And a great windstorm arose, and the waves beat into the boat, so that it was already filling. But He was in the stern, asleep on a pillow. And they awoke Him and said to Him, "Teacher, do You not care that we are perishing?" Then He arose and rebuked the wind, and said to the sea, "Peace, be still!" And the wind ceased and there was a great calm. But He said to them, "Why are you so fearful? How is it that you have no faith?" And they feared exceedingly, and said to one another, "Who can this be, that even the wind and the sea obey Him!"

Mark 4:35–41 (NKJV)

Throughout this book, I have given you practical steps and ways to apply God's Word to the challenging circumstances you will encounter in your life. But everything you do must

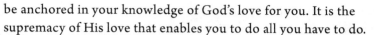

be anchored in your knowledge of God's love for you. It is the supremacy of His love that enables you to do all you have to do.

To discuss this principle of the supremacy of God's love for us, let us examine the Gospel of Mark, the fourth chapter, verses 35–41. This sea crossing experience was so significant and life-changing for the disciples that, along with Mark, Matthew, and Luke, also documented the occurrence, with some slight variations. However, all three accounts say Jesus was asleep when the storm arose, and the disciples began to panic. I believe the fact that Jesus was resting during a time of what looked like an imminent disaster and probable death for the disciples was a major point that our Father would want us to grasp and understand fully.

Jesus had told the disciples they were going to the other side. He said to them, "Let *us* cross over," indicating that everyone was going to get to the other side. But a storm arose during the crossing, and the disciples were, no doubt, frantically working, trying to overcome the desperate situation. I suppose some were bailing water out as it filled the boat, and others were rowing, trying to keep on the right course and keep the boat from capsizing and sinking into the sea. No doubt they were dismayed and maybe even angry because Jesus had the audacity to be asleep, appearing not to care that they were about to go under.

It is as though they didn't know who He was. They had walked with Him, talked with Him, broken bread with Him, and traveled with Him. They had witnessed many miracles such as lepers being cleansed and made whole, the blind made to see, the mute enabled to talk, the lame made to walk, run, and jump, and demons exorcised, just to name a few miraculous events. But they still did not comprehend the vastness, the fullness of who He was. That's why they exclaimed, "Who can this be, that even the wind and the sea obey Him!" The King James Version of the Bible says they exclaimed, "What manner of man is this?"

His sleeping should have signified to them that they were going to be okay. But let us not so quickly judge the disciples. I have to admit that on occasions, I have panicked and questioned what seemed to be Jesus's ignoring of my chaotic, desperate predicaments.

There have been times in my life when I cried out to the Lord about a situation, and He seemed to be asleep, not paying attention. However, since I know He never sleeps nor slumbers (Psalms 121:4), His silence should have indicated to me that He had everything under control. But just like the disciples, I panicked and sometimes questioned His love for me. I was doing everything I knew to do: praying, fasting, studying, consecration time, and attending every service; in other words, working frantically, trying to work it out myself and not depending on Him.

And then, one day, I was expressing this to my campus pastor, and he told me, "Rev. Allen, there comes a time when you just have to rest in the supremacy of God's love. You just have to trust that He's got you. He loves you. You can't work it out. You're depending on what you are doing and not on His love for you." That was a "wow" moment for me!

As I left that encounter, I continued to think about what the Pastor said over the next few days and weeks, and I prayed for the Holy Spirit to illuminate a greater understanding for me. One day I was thinking about when I was a little girl and going to church. The first song I remember learning was "Jesus loves me, this I know, for the Bible tells me so." Over and repeatedly, the Word of God expresses His great love toward us.

He knows the storms are coming. He knows the trials that await you, but He also knows that His love for you is going to cause you to triumph over every challenge. That's why He is resting, seated, sitting at the right hand of the Father, calm and composed, and if He is seated and resting, so should we be. We are in Him, and everything that He is, we *are*, by grace, through faith.

There is no surer, no firmer foundation than the love of God, and God wants us to live in this supernatural resting place in His love. Listen to Ephesians 3:14–19 (NKJV):

For this reason, I kneel before the Father, from whom every family in heaven and on earth derives its name. I pray that out of his glorious riches he may strengthen you with power through his Spirit in your inner being, so that Christ may dwell in your hearts through faith. And I pray that you, being rooted and established in love, may have power, together with all the Lord's holy people, to grasp how wide and long and high and deep is the love of Christ, and to know this love that surpasses knowledge—that you may be filled to the measure of all the fullness of God.

Paul prays first that God, with His endless resources, would grant us inner strengthening in our present experiences; in other words, whatever we are going through. As a result of this inner strengthening, this empowering, Christ assumes full Lordship in every area of our lives, resting, ruling, and abiding with us as the governing authority in our attitudes and conduct. We begin to think and respond from a Christ perspective.

Paul bases his second petition on the fact that believers have already been placed in the body of Christ by His great love for us, demonstrated by His death on the cross. Paul's prayer is that we might be empowered to fully comprehend the vastness of Christ's love and to recognize that love in our personal, day-to-day experiences.

He loves you, and that undermines and supersedes everything contrary to His love.

What is the evidence that He loves you? How do you know He loves you? Because if the enemy could have taken you out by now, out of your purpose, out of your destiny, out of your mind, out of this life, he would have. Make no mistake about it: the enemy hates you! He is neither ambivalent nor uncommitted concerning you. He hates you and works diligently to trick you into death. But the supremacy of God's love for you overwhelms, overcomes, overrules, and overrides the tactics of the enemy. So, rest in His love!

By faith, enter His rest (Hebrews 4:1–3). By faith, keep doing what you do. Pray, study to show yourself approved, fast sometimes just to keep your flesh in submission, take a day every now and then and stay off the internet and other social media sources and just read the Word.

You may be saying to yourself, "Why do I need to keep *doing* stuff when I'm resting?" Because what you *do* demonstrates your faith in His love. What you do demonstrates your faith in what Christ accomplished on the Cross. The Word of God tells us faith without works (doing) is dead (James 2:20). Your faith is activated and comes alive by your actions. Your faith is not in your works but in His love. And so when it appears that nothing is happening, nothing is changing, keep doing those things within the context of the knowledge of His love for you. First and foremost, be diligent to enter that rest (Hebrews 4:11), be quick to rely on, depend upon, bank on, brag on, be assured of, and rest in the supremacy of God's love for you, which was demonstrated by what Christ accomplished on the cross.

God loves you, and His love for you eclipses every mistake, bad decision, wrong choice, and idiotic move you have ever made or will make! His love for you is bigger than, better than, and stronger than anything wrong you might do or that might be done to you, and His love has a greater impact than anything else in your life!

Further evidence of His love for us is what the Word says. John 3:16 says that He loves us so much that He gave His only Son to die for us. Romans 5:8 says that while we were still sinners—not after we got it right, not after we were trying to do better, but while we were wretched—Christ died for us!

How do I know He loves me? Because my enemies have not consumed me, they have *not* triumphed over me (Psalm 41:11).

God loves you. That supersedes every fear, every situation, and every challenge you will ever face. However, the question with which we are faced is this: *How do we rest in this knowledge of His love?*

We do so by remembering!

Remember: we have a high priest who can sympathize with our weaknesses, who identifies with our pain, our fears, and our disappointments. Christ was touched by the feeling of our infirmities in all points, yet He did not sin (Hebrew 4:15). This demonstrates His love, and so we rest.

Remember: the Spirit we received does not make us slaves so that we live in fear; rather, the Spirit we received brought about our adoption to sonship, *made us heirs,* and by Him, we cry, "Abba, Father" (Romans 8:15). This demonstrates His love, and so we rest.

Remember: when we consider that our present sufferings are not worth comparing with the glory that will be revealed in us (Romans 8:18), this demonstrates His love, and so we rest.

Remember: the Spirit helps us in our weakness. We do not know what we should pray for, but the Spirit himself intercedes for us through groans that words cannot express (Romans 8:26). This demonstrates His love, and so we rest.

Remember that in all things, God works for the good of those who love Him, who have been called according to his purpose (Romans 8:28). This demonstrates His love, and so we rest.

Remember that those He predestined, He also called; those He called, He also justified; those He justified, He also glorified. What, then, shall we say in response to these things? If God is for us, who can be against us? (Romans 8:29–31). This demonstrates His love, and so we rest.

The Word of God clearly and convincingly tells us that neither trouble nor hardship or persecution or famine or nakedness or danger or sword shall separate us from the love of God, which is in Christ Jesus. As a matter of fact, in all these things, we are more than conquerors through Him who loves us (Romans 8:35–39).

Even at your best, you will come up short, but His love never fails. So, when you mess up, start to worry, forget, or even sin, first, *repent* and then go right back to resting in His love. You might say something like, "God, I know You love me. You've proven it time and time again. You care about what happens to me. You love me so much that You say there is nothing that can separate me from your love, and so I rest in Your great love for me. I'm settled, I'm sure, I'm confident in Your love for me. I know I don't deserve it. That's what makes it so special, so wonderful, and wondrous, and gracious."

Our heavenly Father knows that the enemy of the saints will always trouble us and try to make us believe in ourselves and our own strength. When we do this, we will surely fail. But when we depend on the love of Christ, we find ourselves in a position of strength and power, not ours but His. And in His strength, power, and love, we can do all that we need to do!

Remember, He paid a debt He did not owe because we owed a debt we could not pay. That's love! Remember, He died a cruel, brutal death on the cross for our sins. That's love! They placed Him in a borrowed tomb. He went to hell and back, took captivity captive, but on the third day, He got up, providing resurrection and redemption power for us. That's love!

Remember: He got up and then ascended into heaven. And now He sits at the right hand of the Father, advocating at all times and in all things on our behalf. This demonstrates His love for us, and so we rest.

His love for us takes precedence over and makes null and void everything contrary to it, *so rest in the supremacy of His love!*

Action Item

Conduct a word search in your Bible for "the love of God," "the love of the Lord," "the love of Christ," and choose a different scripture every week and meditate on it.

If you are feeling especially challenged, read Romans 8:35–39.

Prayer

Gracious God, thank You for loving me no matter how unlovely I can be. You are truly my Abba, Father. Holy Spirit, remind me of Your love for me so that I can rest no matter what is going on in my life. And help me demonstrate Your love to others. In Jesus's name, I pray. Amen.

Reflections

thrive

Chapter 9

SELF-CARE

Flee sexual immorality. Every sin that a man does is outside the body, but he who commits sexual immorality sins against his own body. Or do you not know that your body is the temple of the Holy Spirit who is in you, whom you have from God, and you are not your own? For you were bought at a price; therefore, glorify God in your body and in your spirit, which are God's.

1 Corinthians 6:18–20 (NKJV)

No matter how often I travel by plane, I always pay attention to the flight attendant's safety instructions. Those instructions are intended to give you the greatest chance of survival if there are any difficulties or unexpected occurrences during the flight. The one instruction that sticks out to me every time concerns the oxygen masks. If the mask falls, it is an indication that the oxygen level has changed in the cabin, and breathing may be difficult. If this occurs, you are instructed to put your mask on first before trying to help anyone else. The first time I heard this instruction, after becoming a mother, I thought, *I'm putting my child's mask on first.*

I have since come to understand that if I am having trouble breathing, I will likely be unable to help anyone else, even my own child. That's why I need to make sure my mask is on first, not just for me but for anyone else I care about who may be depending on me. If I can't breathe, I can't help anyone else. This is the principle of self-care.

Purpose of Self-Care

The purpose of self-care is to be physically, mentally, emotionally, and spiritually healthy and strong in order to give God our best service. We must abstain from anything and anyone that hinders a healthy lifestyle. Conversely, we must engage in and embrace those things that promote healthy living.

If you are saved, your body is a temple where the Holy Spirit resides. You are obligated to take care of it, to take care of yourself. Based on the Lord's instructions through Paul in 1 Corinthians, self-care is not an option; it is a mandate.

Whether considering the physical, emotional, mental, or spiritual aspects of ourselves, there are some obvious dangers to avoid, such as sexual immorality, illicit drugs, alcohol, tobacco, the excess of food, and other substances that lead to addictions, which lead to hazardous behaviors. Whether alone or keeping company with those who indulge in any of these things, it is unhealthy and risky and may lead to catastrophic consequences for you.

Yes, there are some obvious glaring dangers that sabotage self-care. But there are some not-so-obvious things we do or fail to do for ourselves that are just as dangerous and hinder our witness for the Lord.

I have identified four categories of self-care and some of the dangers I have encountered and associated with them. This is not a comprehensive list, but it includes those I consider to be a priority. They are intended to stimulate your thinking and maybe identify other areas important for you.

Let's consider them by category:

Physically

- Not getting enough sleep
- Little or no exercise
- Not eating properly; too much of the wrong foods
- Not getting an annual physical examination
- Not getting an annual dental examination
- Not following the advice of the medical professionals

Emotionally

- Allowing negative people to invade your space
- Not guarding your heart
- Not getting counseling/therapy when needed

Mentally

- Watching too much TV
- Engaging in too much social media
- Not consuming enough inspiring/stimulating books, programs, music, etc.
- Not getting counseling/therapy when needed
- Knowing when to say no

I work diligently to not expose myself to people or situations that cause me to have ungodly thoughts that may lead to ungodly behavior. I reserve the right to just say no! When it is unavoidable, I pray inwardly and speak only when necessary.

Spiritually

- Failure to pray regularly (1 Thessalonians 5:17)

- Failure to read the Bible regularly (2 Timothy 3:16)

- Failure to study the Word regularly (James 1:21–25)

- Failure to read and study other spiritual, biblically based books

- Failure to fast (Mark 9:29)

- Failure to worship (Psalm 29:2)

- Failure to attend church service (Hebrews 10:24–25)

- Failure to fellowship with the saints consistently (Hebrews 10:24–25)

- Failure to serve (Matthew 9:35)

- Failure to give (Malachi 3:10)

It is not selfish to take care of yourself. On the contrary, it demonstrates your obedience to the Word of God to glorify Him in your body and spirit (1 Corinthians 6:20). It is the commitment to value the temple where the Holy Spirit lives.

When you consider the above areas I cited and maybe add more or different ones of your own, the thought of self-care may be somewhat daunting. It was for me a few years ago when I realized I was not taking good care of myself. I asked the Lord how I could possibly do everything I needed to do in all these areas and still fulfill all my other responsibilities. The answer for me was to develop a plan. To write down what I needed to do in each area and to schedule it into my life. I had to be purposeful and determined to put myself first and not feel guilty about it.

Initially, it was a struggle to schedule self-care items into my routine, and then I realized that everything was not a daily event. Some things would be daily, but others would be weekly, monthly, or another time frame designation.

Develop a Self-Care Plan

The Bible tells us that Christ often went off by himself to rest and pray and reflect (Matthew 6, 14).

For my physical self-care:

- I exercise five to six days a week. I do four days of the treadmill and two days of resistance training.

- I see my doctors regularly.

- I have at least two dental visits yearly.

- I am making a very focused effort to eat more vegetables and smaller portions of everything else.

- For my spiritual self-care:

- I pray daily.

- I have regular private Bible study time. Currently, I'm studying Colossians.

- I regularly attend corporate worship services and Bible study at my church.

- I regularly read Bible-based, spiritual books.

- I regularly have a day of consecration. On this day, I very purposefully avoid any television, social media, phone calls, etc. If I watch television, it is carefully selected biblical/inspirational programming that can be found on any of the Christian stations. Or I listen to praise and worship music all day. Throughout the course of the day, I pray or read Scripture as directed by the Holy Spirit. As much as possible, I don't engage in any "worldly" activities. I try to spend the entire day (about fourteen to sixteen hours) just meditating on the things of God.

For my emotional/mental health:

- I travel for pleasure as much as possible.

- I read a lot. I am especially fond of historical and biographical material.

- I regularly journal. This has proven to be a very effective stress reliever for me.

- I attend therapy/counseling.

- When I encounter negativity, I try to immediately perform a positive act.

Finally, for all three health areas, I have found that spontaneously stopping throughout the course of the day to praise the Lord is extremely beneficial. So, I very purposefully do this at least once a day.

I want to end this chapter by posing some questions for you to consider over the next few days. They are:

Have you given the idea of self-care serious thought in the past three months?

If yes, did something specific happen that caused you to do so? Explain.

Do you think self-care is important? If yes, why?

If not, why not?

When was the last time you had an annual physical examination?

How long has it been since you read your Bible?

How long has it been since you read any other book?

What are your thoughts about going to a therapist/counselor?

It might be helpful to write your responses down for further reflection.

Action Item(s)

Identify the areas you need to take better care of yourself and be completely honest. After all, this is just between you and the Lord. Next, decide on one of those areas to address immediately. Next, identify one problem in that area. Identify two things you can do to address the specific problem. For example, if you identify you are lacking in physical self-care because you have gained weight, you might decide to engage in some form of exercise for thirty minutes at least three days a week. You might also decide to omit or drastically decrease some particularly harmful food from your diet, i.e., soda.

In a month, address another problem in that same area of self-care or address another area. Follow the same steps above until you are addressing every area of self-care you have identified.

Prayer

Dear Father, I commit every area of my life to You, especially those areas where I am not doing a good job of taking care of myself.

I believe what Your Word says: that my body is the temple where Holy Spirit lives. I want to be the best I can be in order to do all you have for me to do. Holy Spirit, help me to identify and address those areas where I am not doing well. I need Your guidance and strength. In Jesus's name, I pray. Amen!

Reflections

thrive

Chapter 10

BENEDICTION

Now may the God of peace who brought up our Lord Jesus from the dead, that great Shepherd of the sheep, through the blood of the everlasting covenant, make you complete in every good work to do His will, working in you what is well pleasing in His sight, through Jesus Christ, to whom be glory forever and ever. Amen.

Hebrews 13:20–21 (NKJV)

*W*hen I decided to go back to school to get my doctorate degree, someone asked why I felt it necessary to get more education. The tone of the person's voice and his overall demeanor made me feel as if he was criticizing me.

At the time, it was difficult for me to put into words the deep need I had to learn more. I clumsily paraphrased 2 Timothy 2:15: "Be diligent to present yourself approved to God, a worker who does not need to be ashamed, rightly dividing the word of truth." I then tried to explain that in order for me to rightly divide the truth, I needed to know more. However, I failed to fully explain the desire I had inside of me concerning the need for more *knowledge* because I didn't quite understand why myself.

Two years later, I was reading *The Weight of Glory* by C. S. Lewis. In his sermon entitled "Learning in Wartime," I found his discussion of the pursuit of knowledge and beauty. He said:

> I mean the pursuit of knowledge and beauty, in a sense, for their own sake, but in a sense which does not exclude their being for God's sake. An appetite for these things exists in the human mind, and God makes no appetite in vain. We can therefore pursue knowledge as such, and beauty as such, in the sure confidence that by so doing we are either advancing to the vision of God ourselves or indirectly helping others to do so.[15]

As I read this, I uttered a victorious exclamation to no one in particular, "Yes!" I was overwhelmed with a sense of gratitude and relief for Lewis's eloquent expression of what I felt. His words validated my desire to see the Sistine Chapel and the Grand Canyon and get my PhD. To date, I have seen the Grand Canyon and obtained my doctorate degree.

I am compelled to pursue excellence, strive, and learn more. I have searched my heart. I have been brutally honest with myself. For my peace of mind, I *have* to know that my pursuit is not for vain glory or prideful recognition from the world. My pursuit of excellence is the way in which I press toward the mark of the high calling that is in Christ Jesus (Philippians 3:14). For me, it is applying the Word of God to my life; being obedient to the Word of God. For me, it is not to sin intentionally, and if my best is as filthy rags before Him (Isaiah 64:6), anything less than my best is intentional sin.

I pursue excellence because it is my reasonable service to offer my body as a living sacrifice. For me, "offering my body" is doing my best in all things at all times (Romans 12:1). My best is required. It demonstrates my faith in God, my belief that He will do exceedingly, abundantly above all I hope or imagine (Ephesians 3:20).

I do so for my ancestors. They were more talented than I, wiser than I, stronger than I, and more righteous than I. They had greater faith than I have demonstrated, and yet they were confined, constrained, and crippled by the times they lived in. I owe it to my parents, grandparents, great-grandparents, etc., to be the best I can be and to achieve all that I can because they were not allowed to live up to their fullest potential.

I pursue excellence for my descendants: my children, grandchildren, great-grandchildren, etc., and all those who will come after me. They will have more and greater opportunities. They will rise higher than I can imagine. I owe it to them to set an example, no matter how inadequate that example might be. And so, as one of my young spiritual daughters said to me, "I go hard in the paint!" It demonstrates my faith that God will do greater in my life. *It is thriving in the midst!*

I said all that to say this: Do not be discouraged, disheartened, or dissuaded as you pursue excellence. There will be those who don't understand why you feel it necessary. Your pursuit of excellence will identify others who are pursuing excellence, as well as those who embrace the mediocre. There will be those who think you think you are better than them because you want to know and do and have and experience more than they desire. You desire *greater*. You believe God for *greater*. This is alarming and intimidating to the insecure, but I say to you: go for it, believe God, do your best, keep moving and growing and learning and teaching and mentoring. Never do just enough! It is beneath you and the mighty, great God you serve. God is for you. He loves you! So don't just survive but thrive in the midst of every challenge you face!

A benediction is a prayer for God's blessing or an affirmation that God's blessing is at hand.[16] I believe you are positioned for God's blessings in your life, and so I end by giving you some of my favorite Scriptures of benediction.

According to Numbers 6:25–26 (NKJV):

"The Lord bless you and keep you; the Lord make His face shine upon you, and be gracious to you; the Lord lift up His countenance upon you, and give you peace."

According to Ephesians 3:20–21 (NKJV):

Now to Him who is able to do exceedingly abundantly above all that we ask or think, according to the power that works in us, to Him be glory in the church by Christ Jesus to all generations, forever and ever. Amen.

According to Hebrews 13:20–21 (NKJV):

Now may the God of peace who brought up our Lord Jesus from the dead, that great Shepherd of the sheep, through the blood of the everlasting covenant, make you complete in every good work to do His will, working in you what is well pleasing in His sight, through Jesus Christ, to whom be glory forever and ever. Amen.

According to Jude 24–25 (NKJV):

Now to Him who is able to keep you from stumbling, and to present you faultless before the presence of His glory with exceeding joy, to God our Savior, who alone is wise, be glory and majesty, dominion and power, both now and forever. Amen.

May this God rest, rule, and abide with you henceforth now and forever more as you thrive to His glory. Amen!

Action Item(s)

Today, actively look for someone who needs encouragement and encourage them. This can be done with a brief conversation witnessing about a challenge the Lord brought you through, or you could send a card or inexpensive gift with a note. Maybe you can take someone to lunch or invite them to your home for tea and fellowship. Make yourself available to be used by God.

Prayer

Holy Father, I marvel at Your mercy, I meditate on Your magnificence, I contemplate Your creativity, I worship Your wonderfulness, I praise Your perfection, I glorify Your goodness, I am in awe of Your awesomeness, and I celebrate Your sovereignty. When I consider Your holiness, it causes me to look at myself, and I realize how unworthy I am. When I think about how You love me, knowing how unlovable I can be, my heart cries out in complete gratitude. Thank You, Father, hallelujah!

I am humbled by Your holiness; I am strengthened by Your steadfastness; I am encouraged by Your enlightening; I am made bold by Your strength, and I know that I can do all things through You. You are my Creator, my Savior, my Healer, my Deliverer. You are my strong tower, my banner, my strength, and my help. You are my provider, my joy, my peace, my comfort, my hope, my friend, my Lord, and my God. All that I am or ever hope to be is in You. Thank You, God, that you empower me to thrive and pursue excellence to Your glory. Hallelujah and amen!

Reflections

PRAYER OF SALVATION

I am compelled to offer those of you who don't know this God I have talked about the opportunity to come to know Him. Please read this prayer aloud:

Heavenly Father, I know that I am a sinner and that I need Jesus in my life. I believe Jesus died for my sins, was raised from the dead, and is alive. Please forgive me of my sins and come into my life and save me. In Jesus's name, I pray. Amen.

Hallelujah, and welcome to new life!

I encourage you to find a Bible-based church in which to learn more about your heavenly Father, who you are in Christ, and how to live this new life to the fullest.

Miracles and Blessings

Rev. Dr. Caron M. Allen

NOTES

[1]   Dr. Cynthia Hale, *I'm a Piece of Work! Sisters Shaped by God* (Valley Forge, PA: Judson Press, 2010).

[2]   *Merriam-Webster.com Dictionary*, s.v. "inheritance," accessed September 7, 2022, www.merriam-webster.com/dictionary/inheritance.

[3]   *Merriam-Webster.com Dictionary*, s.v. "thrive," accessed September 7, 2022, www.merriam-webster.com/dictionary/thrive.

[4]   Eileen Patten, "Racial, gender wage gaps persist in U.S. despite some progress," Pew Research Center, July 1, 2016, www.pewresearch.org/fact-tank/2016/07/01/racial-gender-wage-gaps.

[5]   *Merriam-Webster Collegiate Dictionary, Eleventh Edition* (Springfield, MA: Merriam-Webster, Incorporated, 2004), s.v "success."

[6]   Caron Barton Allen, *From Whence They Came; the Genealogical History of an African American Family* (Baltimore, MD: PublishAmerica, 2009).

[7]   Steven Covey, *The 7 Habits of Highly Effective People* (New York: Fireside, Simon & Schuster, Inc., 1989).

[8]   James Dixon II, *Unleash Your Faith-Unlock God's Power* (Charlotte, NC: LifeBridge Books, 2009).

[9]   *Merriam-Webster.com Dictionary*, s.v. "mantra," accessed September 7, 2022, www.merriam-webster.com/dictionary/mantra.

[10]   *Merriam-Webster Collegiate Dictionary, Eleventh Edition* (Springfield, MA: Merriam-Webster, Incorporated, 2004), s.v. "tension."

[11]   Bishop Dr. Jackie L. Green, *When She Hears the Call* (Redlands, CA: JGM International Prayer Life Institute).

[12]   Brady Boyd, *Let Her Lead* (Colorado Springs, CO: CreateSpace Independent Publishing Platform, 2014).

[13]   *Merriam-Webster's Collegiate Dictionary, Eleventh Edition,* (Springfield, MA: Merriam-Webster, Incorporated, 2004), s.v. "to abandon."

14   *Merriam-Webster's Collegiate Dictionary, Eleventh Edition,* (Springfield, MA: Merriam-Webster Incorporated, 2004), s.v. "dross."

15   C. S. Lewis, *Complete Works of C.S. Lewis* (Strelbytskyy Multimedia Publishing, 2021), https://books.google.com/books?id=31DuDwAAQBAJ, p. 3,821.

16   *The Concise Holman Bible Dictionary* (Nashville, TN: Broadman & Holman Publishers, 1997, 2001).

SUGGESTED READING

From Whence They Came; the Genealogical History of an African-American Family by Dr. Caron M. Allen

Matters of the Heart by Dr. Juanita Bynum

Let Her Lead by Brady Boyd

The Seven Habits of Highly Effective People by Stephen R. Covey

The Beautiful Battle by Mary E. DeMuth

The Difference is Vision by Bishop James Dixon

Unleash Your Faith, Unlock God's Power by Bishop James Dixon

If God Is So Good, Why Are Blacks Doing So Bad? by Bishop James Dixon

The Hour That Changes the World by Dick Eastman

Theology You Can Count On by Tony Evans

Tony Evans' Book of Illustrations by Tony Evans

Purpose for Everyday Living by Criswell Freeman

When She Hears the Call by Bishop Jackie Green

I'm a Piece of Work by Dr. Cynthia Hale

The Walk at Work by Andria Hall

Seeing Jesus by Marilyn Hickey

Love Dare by Steven and Alex Kendrick with Lawrence Kimbrough

When Women Walk Alone; Finding Strength and Hope through the Seasons of Life by Cindi McMenamin

Battlefield of the Mind by Joyce Meyer

The Power of Positive Thoughts by Joyce Meyer

Power of a Praying Wife by Stormie Omartian

Power of a Praying Woman by Stormie Omartian

Leading at the Edge by Dennis N. T. Perkins

Unmerited Favor by Joseph Prince

The Cross of Christ by John R. W. Stott

The Wife's Role by Robb D. Thompson
40 Day Soul Fast by Dr. Cindy Trimm
The Rules of Engagement by Dr. Cindy Trimm
The Leadership Gap by Curtis Wallace
Prayer of Jabez by Dr. Bruce H. Wilkinson

CONTACT INFORMATION

Dr. Allen would love to hear your thoughts on *In Christ, I Thrive*. Please send your comments to thrivinginthemidst2017@gmail.com or visit the website at www.thrivinginthemidst.org.

Dr. Allen can be engaged to address the following topics: ministry organization, ministry leadership, church security, and career development. For preaching, teaching, conducting conferences, or book signings, Dr. Allen can be reached at:

(904) 395–7450

thrivinginthemidst2017@gmail.com

OTHER BOOKS BY DR. ALLEN

*From Whence They Came; the Genealog-
ical History of an African American Family*

Thriving in the Midst: A Devotional for 20/20 Vision

Thrive in Five: A Devotional for Forward Motion

A Guide to Fasting

CPSIA information can be obtained
at www.ICGtesting.com
Printed in the USA
BVHW052033200223
658864BV00010B/150